THE COMPLETE
POETRY OF
SAMUEL HOFFENSTEIN

THE COMPLETE POETRY

OF

SAMUEL HOFFENSTEIN

THE MODERN LIBRARY · NEW YORK

First Modern Library Edition, 1954

Copyright, 1923, 1924, 1928, 1930, 1932, 1947, by Samuel Hoffenstein

All Rights Reserved

Library of Congress Catalog Card Number: 54-6895

Random House IS THE PUBLISHER OF *The Modern Library*

BENNETT A. CERF · DONALD S. KLOPFER · ROBERT K. HAAS

Manufactured in the United States of America

Printed by Parkway Printing Company   Bound by H. Wolff

Contents

~~~~~~

Poems in Praise of Practically Nothing

Year In, You're Out

Pencil in the Air

Poems in Praise of Practically Nothing

~~~~~~

TO EDITH MORGAN

Since, as they say, the rare exceptions prove
The rule in life and letters, even love,
The rule of my dispraises seems more true
Because of that most rare exception, you.

Proem

How exquisite my sorrows look
Neatly marshalled in a book,
Hung on the iambic line
In an orderly design!

See how smooth my trouble goes!—
Printer, weep not on my woes,
Lest your sympathetic grief
Make a blot upon the leaf!

Sweetheart, sigh not for the drear
Winter of my spirit's year,
Lest it vanish—and I can't
Manage the trochaic chant!

Let the winds of fortune blow
To the metres that I know:
There are always better times
Waiting to corrupt our rhymes.

Songs to Break the Tedium of Riding a Bicycle, Seeing One's Friends, or Heartbreak

I

Along the country roads there grow
Willow-trees and Texaco,
Mobiloils and marigold
And other fruits of men and mould.
Oh, how my town-tried heart desires
To know the peace of Kelly Tires,
To hear the robin in the grass
Sing, "Socony," as I pass!
Some day I shall fly the rut
And build a small, bucolic hut,
Trim a hedge and hop a stile,
Walk my Camel for a mile,
Milk a mid-Victorian cow—
Eventually, but not now.

II

My luck with the proverbial sex
Should rile, torment me and perplex;
Should turn my simple psyche sour
As, *par exemple*, Schopenhauer.
It should imbue me with disgust
Of women's misproportioned dust;

4

Should make me look, with dubious eye,
On every female passerby:
Suspect the sting, mistrust the buzz—
Well, my lad, it does, it does!

III

When trouble drives me into rhyme,
Which is two-thirds of all the time,
What peace a thought like this can give—
Great is the age in which we live!
My heart is heavy, but I know
They're working on the radio;
That letters, by aerial post,
Go every day from coast to coast.
I may be sunk beyond repair,
Drunk less on liquor than despair,
And yet my heart leaps up when I
Behold *Sweet Caporal* in the sky.
Though winter-bare my solitude,
Though heartbreak in its branches brood,
I know that future wars will be
Fought by super-chemistry,
And, therefore, loneliness and loss
Are but a mask for applesauce;—
For I am lord of life and death,
Who flaunt this flaming shibboleth:—
No matter what the morrow brings,
Inventors are inventing things!

IV

Between the mighty legs of Death
We play the schoolboy pranks of breath:

Scrawl challenge on his sodden boots,
The while he coils his cypress-roots.

V

I do not question Woman's place:
She's entered in the human race;
She has a natural turn of mind
For propagation of her kind;
She is—that is to say, a few—
Fairly decorative too,
And on her once maternal breast—
The vogue is past—men used to rest.
If, in this golden age of dames,
She stalks a few surprising claims,
Attempts to puzzle and perplex
Old Nature with a change of sex,
And tumbles from her ancient shelf
In trying to express herself—
Ah, who am I to bid her stay,
Nor try to shave the Mennen way!
There may be some, whose ways are meek;
Who dream submission to a sheik;
Who'd like to waste their love and care
And sweetness on a desert heir;
Who are not fretting to be free
Of orthodox biology;
(If such there be, go mark one well,
And hold her in some citadel!)
But Woman, as they say in Greece,
Is on the hoof for Bigger Fleece:
Too long a serf, too long oppressed
By butter 'n' egg men from the West,

By whiskered juries, blunt of wit,
Who take two hours to acquit.
I hope she finds her proper niche,
Her why and wherefore, what and which,
For through the town I sadly roam,
And note, her place is not the home.

Verses Demonstrating That No Man Can Be Unhappy Amid the Infinite Variety of This World, and Giving the Reader Choice of Several Titles, the Author's Favorite Being, "Some Play Golf and Some Do Not"

Oh, how various is the scene
Whereon we spend our day!—I mean,
Oh, how various is the scene
Allowed to Man for his demesne!
But let's get on—Hip, hip, hurray-o!
Gloria in excelsis Deo,
Who gave us such variety
That none need discontented be;
That each may find his proper niche:
The poor, the maimed, the wretched rich,
The saint (ha, ha!), the son—I mean,
Oh, how various is the scene!—
The earth, whose aspects countless are
As bugs and sneezes in catarrh;
The changeful world so full of things,
From happy deuces down to kings,
That each, no matter how distressed
May find some thing of in-ta-rest.

Consider first topography,
Climate and geography:

8

Here's the land and there's the sea;
Here's a hill and there's a valley;
Here's a street and there's an alley;
Here's a mountain capped with snow;
Yon, yes, yon's, a swell plateau;
Here's a forest full of trees;
There's a meadow full of fleas:—
Oh, how various is the scene!
(You know exactly what I mean.)
Here is Paris, there is Rome;
Hither's Newark, thither's Nome;
Here is Kansas, yonder's Cork;
Here is Cairo, there New York;
Here the heathen, slightly bored,
Hymns his freshly-baptized Lord,
There's Detroit and Henry Ford:—
Oh, how various is the scene!—
(You know exactly what I mean.)
Well, here it's cold and there it's hot;
Here it's raining, there it's not;
Here it's north and there it's south;
Yon it's wet, but here, what drouth!
Here the tiger eats raw meat;
There the walrus flaps his feet;
Here it's dark and there it's light;
First comes day, and then comes night;
Here it's solid, yon it's air;
Here it's here, and there it's there:—
Oh, how various is the scene
Allowed to Man for his demesne,
So full of this and that and them,
That living is a perfect gem;

That each, no matter what his lot,
May know it's cold while he is hot;
May rapture find in deepest woe
That there it's high while he is low.

Turn we now the other cheek,
And note how various is the week;
Now it's Thursday, now it's Sunday,
Now it's Friday, now it's Monday—
(Blessed be His lavish ways:
There are even other days!)
Tuesday, Saturday and Friday:—
None is *your* day, none is *my* day;
Each belongs to one and all—
Sick or well or great or small:—
Oh, how various is the scene
Whereon we live—well, what I mean
Is—wretched, poor, or blind, or lame,
Sing we praises to His Name!
Now in ecstasy we trace
The aspects of the human race:
Some are men and some are women;
Some—well, anyhow they're human;
Some are short and some are tall;
Some are big and some are small;
Some are dark and some are fair;
Some are bald and some have hair;
Some have all their teeth, but most
To dentists go and eat milk toast:—
Oh, how various is the scene!—
(You know exactly what I mean.)
Well, some are lean and some are fat;

Some are this and some are that;
Some eat kidneys, some eat frogs;
Some keep horses, some keep dogs;
Some are colored, some are white;
Half are sober, half are tight;
Some wear tweed and some wear serge;
Most have some peculiar urge;
Some have money, some have hives;
Some have hope and some have wives;
Some to crime for profit go;
Some hold office, high and low;
Some have gravel, some have gout;
Some like home, but most go out;
Some are cold and some are hot;
Some play golf and some do not!
Oh, how various is the scene
Allowed to Man for his demesne,
That each, no matter what his blows,
May find a poultice for his woes;
May drive his pains and bills away
With tiger, walrus, night or day;
With north or south or west or east,
Or various kinds of bug and beast;
With Latvia or Rumania,
Greece or Pennsylvania,
Newark, Paris, Akron, Cork,
Cairo, Oslo or New York;
With Tuesday, Wednesday, Friday, Sunday,
Thursday, Saturday or Monday;
With tall or short, or stern or slack,
Or those who like their coffee black;
With those in tweed, or those in serge;

With those who dare, or on the verge;
With cold or hot or fat or lean—
Oh, how various is the scene!—
So full of so and so and so,
That none, come weal or woe, woe, woe,
Amid such swell variety
Can ever discontented be.

Poems of Passion Carefully Restrained
So as to Offend Nobody

~~~~~~~~~~~~~~~~~~~~~~~~~~~~~~~~~~~~~~~

I

You have a most attractive pan,
And I'm a very foolish man,
And, what between the two, I fell
As deep as Dante into hell;
But do you, in your triumph, think
I'll stay forever on the blink,
And pine and pale and waste away
And grow cadaverous and gray—
A wreck, a rum, a shard? Well, maybe
You are right about it, baby!

II

When you're away, I'm restless, lonely,
Wretched, bored, dejected; only
Here's the rub, my darling dear,
I feel the same when you are here.

III

Psycho-analyzed, I stand
And meditate your little hand;
Your lost, evasive eyes, that seem
To lean upon me while they scheme;
And thus contemplative, I know

Why I adore and need you so:—
When I was six or seven or eight,
In that divine, pre-nubile state,
I had a horror, vent in yelpings,
Of what were known as single helpings;
When I was nine, or maybe ten,
I nursed an unrequited yen:
I loved her, middle-aged and shrewish,
That she was Gentile, I but Jewish—
Though now I marvel at it all,
Who am devout Episcopal—
When I was in my 'teens, I dreamed
Green apples were not what they seemed,
But beasts, inimical to rest,
Who sat upon a fellow's chest;
When I achieved the peak of twenty,
Bad breaks with dames I had aplenty,
Who left my burning love behind,
And each, a complex in my mind;—
Now, to these inhibitions true,
I am a-Freud of losing you,
And, though I fully understand,
I meditate your little hand,
Your eyes that lie as like as not,
And love you, whom I ought to swat.

IV

Lovely lady, who does so
All my waking haunt,
Tell me, tell me, do you know
What the hell you want?

Lady, to whose feet I'd bring
The world, if I could win it,
Are you sure of anything
For a single minute?

You whose eyes can kindle flame
Only Death could smother,
Tell me, please, does any dame
Differ from another?

Was the apple applesauce
Eve ate in the garden?
Aren't you all a total loss?
No? I beg your pardon!

V

Oh, the first kiss is sweet—
Like a bud, like a wafer;
But the last, I repeat,
But the last kiss is safer.

The first kiss is sweet
With an innocent savor;
But the last is like meat
With some salt for its flavor.

Oh, with wonder I look—
You so fair, so capricious!
Say, whose goose did you cook
For a meat so delicious?

15

VI

Come, my sweet (or what you will)
Let us drink our blasé fill;
Let us give the night and day
To love and neurasthen-i-ay.

Let our nerves and passions rage
In the manner of the age,
Dancing through erotic scenes
To the jazzing endocrines.

You love me and I love you
And a dozen others too;
Let's exchange, with linkèd hopes,
Our amorous kaleidoscopes.

While the Fords the land obscure,
And radio makes the silence poor,
Let us be exhibit Z
In the new pathology.

VII

Belovèd, let our love be quite
Intense and splendid, but polite,
That in the hour of parting, we
May end the matter pleasantly.

Since the foredoomed farewell is core
Of all the mortal evermore,
Let us not mar with present fret
The gracious sequel of regret.

16

Rather, my little love, let me
Your guide for future lovers be,
Whose pleasure now is sometimes fraught
With envy of the men who taught.

VIII

I cannot elude you, I cannot escape:
You haunt me in every conceivable shape;—
You're morning and midnight and twilight
    and noon,
Orion, the Dipper, the Lion, the moon.

You keep me enchanted, exalted and true
In snares of the fair and ubiquitous you;
I don't mind your being the glories above—
But here you intrude on the ladies I love!

IX

I wish my mind would let me take
You as you are for your own sake;
A trifle less I might adore,
But then, I should enjoy you more.

But Imagination will
Change and transfigure you, until
I never see you, but it seems
Some glory of you stayed in dreams.

Sometimes I think the only thing
That can the lasting rapture bring,
Is not to see you, but to stay
In love with you and far away.

This is the kind of distant bliss
That Dante got from Beatrice:
A woman singing in the trees
A name, an epic, to the breeze.

And men and women all will prove
This cruel arson, against Love—
That he burns all else away
In the belovèd but the clay.

X

Sweetling, try not to forget,
Lest in trying, you remember;
She who blows too hard may get
Flame from the deceptive ember.

Let the attic of your mind
Keep whatever stores are in it;
Do not look too much behind,
Lest you tread the present minute.

I shall pluck the moments now—
Only folly weeps to miss one;
Let some later lover's brow
Wrinkle at the thought of this one!

XI

The rain that falls upon my heart
And on my eyes so wistfully,
Will fall again; I shall not start,
For it will drop so restfully

On eyes that will be pools of quiet,
Upon a heart that will not stir
At memories of ancient riot
Within the rain's sad dulcimer.

Even as it falls upon the ground,
Nor makes the tiniest pebble start,
The rain will fall, nor make a sound
Of anything within my heart—

Neither of the bitter nor the sweet
Of loving you, my dear, my dear—
Though all our moments it repeat,
I, who have loved you, shall not hear.

I shall but stare upon my heaven
Of silent earth and starless stone,
Beyond which, grazing sheep at even
Find peace no greater than my own.

And I, who love you now, my dear,
So wildly that my heart is spent,
Think of the time I shall not hear
Your voice in rain, and am content.

XII

I shall sing a song to you,—
Fair a song as any;
Perfect as a drop of dew—
Rare among the many.

Eager, dancing words will do
Their melodious duty;
Make a lucent mirror, true
To your shining beauty.

I shall coin your golden hair
For a stanza's treasure;
Tame your wild and wayward air
To my love-sick measure.

I shall lift my song and sing
With the voice of doom
The utter loneliness you bring
Into this little room.

Psalm

~~~~~~

High in His holy spires sits the Lord;
He is the bell, the clapper and the cord,
And, taller than the haughty traffic towers,
He sprinkles chimes on the congested hours;
Yet near in lovingkindness to the ground,
He breaks the Sabbath—with His fruitful sound.

Benign and Undenominational,
His benisons from myriad belfries fall:
No special steeples His affections hold,
And styles of architecture leave Him cold;
The stately Gothic in the city fogs,
The shingle Baptist in the rural bogs,
The tricky Moorish, surly Muscovite,
Are equally His dwellings and delight.

With sweet democracy, He plays upon
The simple bell, orchestral carillon,
That he who runs may listen, if not read,
To clangor suited to his secret need,
And know, in toil or wedlock, woe or fear
That God is ever present in his ear.

He is the bell, the clapper and the cord;
The sacerdotal brokers on the board;
The cost of maintenance, the preacher's hire,

The congregation and agnostic choir;
He is, in short, the works, the church entire,
Electing thus, in stone and wood to stand,
That we His love might readily command,
Who else had power, amid divine acclaim,
To call each cherub by her Christian name.

Oh, mighty abnegation, how you shame
My simple sorrows even out of name!
Who but the Lord such sacrifice could make—
To dwell in bishops for his brother's sake?
Who else desert the lovely seraphim,
To be a hallelujah and a hymn,
Or stand, for thankless mankind, year on year,
High Church in London, neo-Jewish here?

Ring out, ring out, ye non-sectarian chimes!
Inspire these pseudo-democratic times!
From Coast to Coast (or even further) roll
Your living Esperanto of the soul!—
The Methodist, anticipating hell,
Is saved from madness by a Baptist bell;
A complex caught in a Semitic brain
A Presbyterian clapper cures again;
And many a Christian Scientist's despair,
When acidosis was still new to prayer,
Was exorcised by brave St. Patrick's peal,
The uric acid flying at its heel,
Because the rival belfry had the grace
Of therapy in his peculiar case.

Oh Lord, I cannot praise too loftily
Your distribution of Divinity;

Ubiquitous, accessible and free,
Benevolent, beneficent and wise;
Each church, Yourself, and of Yourself a guise,
Yourself in all, and yet all different,
To suit the varied need and temperament;—
Sweet stations set along the path of strife,
The via dolorosa of this life.
The melancholy of insolvent days
The Synagogue Emanu-el allays;
And bright St. Thomas, flawless as a rose,
Is my specific for domestic woes;
St. John, that lifts a hummock to a hill,
Whose dome the Lord expands Himself to fill,
Distinctively and obviously divine,
Protects my teeth above the danger line.
And so the blessed catalogue goes on
Through brick and stone and bell and carillon;
The mystic and eternal ministry
That suits each need and each calamity.
High in His holy spires sits the Lord;
He is the bell, the clapper and the cord;
The seventy-thousand aches and pains and needs;
The twenty-thousand therapeutic creeds;
The church, the book, the candles and the chimes;
The Author of my reason and these rhymes.

Poems Intended to
Incite the Utmost Depression

~~~~~~~~~~~~~~~~~~~~~~~~~~~~~~~~~~

I

When love, at last, had left me quiet,
And my heart was clear of pain,
Toxins, due to faulty diet,
Broke it right in two again.

Those who forge our fates above,
Little heed the hurt they do—
Now with toxins, now with love,
They break our trusting hearts in two.

II

Cervantes, Dostoievsky, Poe,
Drained the dregs and lees of woe;
Gogol, Beethoven and Keats
Got but meager share of sweets;
Milton, Homer, Dante, had
Reason to be more than sad;
Cæsar and Napoleon
Saw the blood upon their sun;
Martyr, hermit, saint and priest
Lingered long at Sorrow's feast:
Paid with pyre and perishing
For every feather in each wing;—

Well, if such as these could be
So foredoomed to misery,
And Fate despise her own elect—
What the deuce do *you* expect?

III

You have dreamed, enduring sorrow,
Of a time yclept tomorrow,
When, your share of trouble spent,
You would flower in content,
Trust your woman, sleep till noon,
Keep your teeth and grab the moon:—
Well, tomorrows came your way
And behaved just like today;
Came in droves and caravans
And thumbed their bugles at your plans.
Yet you have the nerve to say,
"Tomorrow is another day,"
And stake your heart upon a boon
From some tomorrow, surnamed Soon.
Incorrigible boob, I hate
Like poison to vaticinate,
But you, who'll never learn a thing,
Listen to the song I sing:
Ere the last tomorrow's gone,
You'll slice moons in Matteawan.

IV

In a million years or so,
Maybe yes and maybe no,
Maybe sooner, like as not,
Sun and stars will go to pot.

They will leave behind no spark:
Earth will curdle in the dark;
Men like women will become,
Adding to their dreadful sum;
A. E. Housman will come back
And take an even gloomier tack.
Nothing I could say or think,
Or fancy, or project in ink,
Would even by one-tenth convey
The horrors of that monstrous day.
And 'tis for this you toil and sweat;
And 'tis for this you moil and fret;
And 'tis for this that men must weep
While women work them while they sleep!
Of course, you say, "A lot I care:—
My heart is weak, I won't be there;
When that time comes, I'll be about
As dead as love the third week out."
Blind oaf, enjoy your vain delight:—
They'll resurrect you just for spite;
They'll haul you from your dreamless bed
To drop a comet on your head.
And 'tis for this you toil and sweat
And moil, et cetera, et cet.,
And wonder if some feeble dame
Still loves her zany, just the same.
Oh, greatest ape that ever was,
I hope she does, I hope she does!

Poems in Praise of Practically Nothing

~~~~~~

I

You buy some flowers for your table;
You tend them tenderly as you're able;
You fetch them water from hither and thither—
What thanks do you get for it all? They wither.

II

Only the wholesomest foods you eat;
You lave and you lave from your head to your feet;
The earth is not steadier on its axis
Than you in the matter of prophylaxis;
You go to bed early and early you rise;
You scrub your teeth and you scour your eyes—
What thanks do you get for it all? Nephritis,
Pyorrhea, appendicitis,
Renal calculus and gastritis.

III

You buy yourself a new suit of clothes;
The care you give it, God only knows;
The material, of course, is the very *best* yet;
You get it pressed and pressed and *pressed* yet;
You keep it free from specks *so* tiny—
What thanks do you get? The pants get shiny.

IV

You practice every possible virtue;
You hurt not a soul, while others hurtue;
You fetch and carry like a market basket—
What thanks do you get for it? Me don't ask it!

V

You leap out of bed; you start to get ready;
You dress and you dress till you feel unsteady;
Hours go by, and still you're busy
Putting on clothes, till your brain is dizzy.
Do you flinch? Do you quit? Do you go out
    naked?—
The least little button, you don't forsake it.
What thanks do you get? Well, for all this mess, yet
When night comes around, you've got to undress yet.

VI

You're kind to women, children, worms;
You speak of God in the highest terms;
You help spell words like "tetrahedral";
You show respect for a cathedral;
You're sweet and gentle as a mouse is:
(Wives should behave so to their spouses!)
Though women tempt you, more than plenty,
Your rate is half a girl in twenty;—
In short, from grace you never fell yet—
And what do you get? On all sides hell yet!

VII

Your life's a wreck; you're tired of living,
Of lending, spending, borrowing, giving;
Of doubt and fear, of hope and question,
Of women, children and digestion;
There isn't a single dream you cherish—
You simply pine and pray to perish.
You haven't the nerve to take bichloride,
But you stay up nights till you're gaunt and sore
    eyed;
You don't eat greens, as the doctors tell you,
And you drink the very worst they sell you;
You've earned, at least, let's say, cirrhosis—
And what do you get for it? Halitosis!

VIII

You take a bath, and sit there bathing
In water cold, in water scathing;
You scrub till you're *sans* an epidermis,
And feel like a regular bathing Hermes.
You do not waste a single minute;
The tub shows how you worked while in it;
You dry, and do some honest rooting
For such remarkable abluting:—
Well, a day goes by, or ten, or thirty,
And what thanks do you get? You're just as dirty!

IX

You meet a girl and you surrender;
Though God knows why, you're kind and tender;
You're husband, lover, sister, brother,

Companion, banker, father, mother;
You try your best to be worthy of her;
You make mistakes, but she knows you love her;
You're hers completely, and you show it:
And what thanks do you get? The gate—I know it!

X

You're a good girl; you're gray with virtue;
The very thought of a misstep hurts you;
You know that honor must be hoarded
Against the day when it is rewarded;
You see a girl who's all men's vassal,
Marry a duke in his own castle;
You see another, who can't say, "No, sir,"
Capture, at least, a wholesale grocer;—
But you never let your thoughts grow sordid:
You know in your heart you'll be rewarded.
Well, the years go by, like queens and roses,
The way they did in the time of Moses,
And what do you get? False teeth, a doorman,
A complex, or assistant foreman!

XI

You hire a cook, but she can't cook yet;
You teach her by candle, bell, and book yet;
You show her, as if she were in her cradle,
Today, the soup, tomorrow, a ladle.
Well, she doesn't learn, so although you need her,
You decide that somebody else should feed her:—
But you're kind by birth; you hate to fire her;
To tell a woman you don't require her—

So you wait and wait, and before you do it,
What thanks do you get? She beats you to it!

XII

You're a pure spirit; you're air and water;
You're nobody's son and nobody's daughter;
In short, you're still in the state pre-natal—
A strange condition, but seldom fatal—
Well, anyhow, you're a harmless atom,
Content to stay in your own stratum;
You do not drink or play the horses,
Or interfere with natural forces,
Indulge in moods or whims erratic,
Which cause the flu, and sometimes, static:—
A perfect type of the homo *non est*,
You're unobtrusive, kind and honest,
As upright as an ear of corn—
And what thanks do you get for it all? You're born!

XIII

You're a positive fiend for life extension:
You eat greens in every dimension;
You know as well as any parrot
The quirks of calory and carrot—
They've taken out, without a quiver,
Your tonsils, teeth, ambition, liver,
Appendix, income—every center
Designed to let bacilli enter.
You never miss the daily dozen
That killed your uncle, brother, cousin;
You breathe only the freshest breezes—
And what do you get? The same diseases.

31

XIV

You work and work, and keep on working,
While poets, even worse, are shirking;
Your hair falls out, your eyes grow bleary,
Your bones grow old, your outlook dreary;
But you never seek to break the fetters—
You go on filing useless letters.
Well, a day arrives, and it must be spring yet:
The birds, somehow, begin to sing yet;
The grass is green, the cows are mooing,
The flies are buzzing, the people shooing,
The air is fresh—it makes you tipsy—
And, all of a sudden, you turn gipsy.
So you come in late, you go home early;
The thought of the office makes you surly;
You come in later, you go home earlier;
The thought of the office makes you surlier;
You've worked enough; you've earned the leisure
To have some poor, but honest pleasure;
No desk, you think, should rise and quell you—
And what do you get? Do I have to tell you?

XV

You go to high school, even college;
You become a regular Book of Knowledge;
You learn that Nero played the fiddle;
That the Sphinx is, after all, a riddle;
That women weep while men go faring;
That Bismarck seldom was a herring.
No matter what a person asks you,

The brilliant answer never tasks you;
You smile and say, "Go ask another,"
Like, "Did the Gracchi have a mother?"
Well, you meet a girl, and nothing sweeter;
The kind—well, anyhow, you meet 'er—
You look her over with elation—
She seems to have a cerebration:
So you start right in, like Kipling's thunder,
To be the twenty-seventh wonder;
You spout such high and fancy learning,
You're sure the girl will die of yearning—
And when you're finished, did you please her?
Did you hear her say, "You're Julius Caesar"?
What thanks did you get? The usual solo:
She likes the Prince of Wales and polo.

XVI

You're born (whose fault is it?) a poet—
Nobody sees it, but you know it;
You try to temper your psychoses
And get, at least, Grade B neuroses;
But it's no use—so great the curse is,
You go from bad to worse, then verses.
But suppose you wrote a poem a minute,
What menace, after all, is in it?
You might have been a chiropractor,
Dentist, diplomat, or actor,
Banker, lawyer, politician,
Or, let us say, your own physician,
Attacked the world, and brought upon it
More harm than even a first-rate sonnet—

Here is your chance, but you eschew it;
You haven't quite the heart to do it—
And what thanks do you get for it? Don't I know
    it?—
You go on being a sap and poet.

Notes for a Superfluous Poem

We chose with care and dined with zest,
A simple fare by genius dressed,
Then home by glittering stars we walked,
And looked on heaven, and gaily talked,
And dreamed a morrow fair as fair,
And drank the bootleg autumn air.
We loved the town for all its bright
Adornment of the naked night,
Its orchid rarities of light.
We loved the town and all its horde,
Whom God has socked but never floored,
And (woe to us!) we loved the Lord.

Then home, and while the night relaxed,
And noises waned, and silence waxed,
We scored against our foes above
That brief perfection which is love.
We took the autumn in and made
A fire for him, and thoughtful shade,
And comfortable at his knees,
We listened to his odysseys,
Until he dropped his misty head,
Was silent. Then we went to bed.

Ah, sequel terrible to tell!
Ah, dreadful sequel that befell!—

Scarce had I tasted slumber's cup,
And scarce prepared on dreams to sup—
An awful nightmare ripped me up!
A nightmare fit for Sisyphus
Leaped up from sizzling Tartarus
And seized me in his brutish paws,
And bit me with his Stygian jaws,
And made a shard, a shred, a patch,
A rag, a wreck, a weed, a thatch,
A heap of dust, a scrap, a bit,
Of all the joys preceding it.

Ah, foe (I quote Millay) and friend,
The moral of this tale attend—
No matter what the Lord may send,
Nightmare gets us in the end.

A Garden of Verses for the Little Ones,
Including Orphans and Step-children, and
Their Parents and Guardians Also

～～～～～～～～～～～～～～～～～～～～～～～～～

I. *Primer*

The camel has a funny hump—
   Well, what of it?
The desert is an awful dump—
   Well, what of it?
The sun it rises every day—
   What about it?
Roosters crow and asses bray—
   What about it?
The stars shine nearly every night—
   Don't bother me with it!
Grass is green and snow is white—
   Get out o' here!

II. *Yes, Dear*

God gave us the blue sky above,
   And I'll forgive Him that.
He made your mother, marriage, love,
   And I'll forgive Him that.
God made the grass, the trees, the dew,
   And I'll forgive Him that.

He also made such boobs as you,
   And that's where He loses out with me!

III. *Lullaby*

Yes, I'll take you to the zoo
To see the yak, the bear, the gnu,
And that's the place where I'll leave you—
   Sleep, little baby!

You'll see the lion in a rage,
The rhino, none the worse for age;
You'll see the inside of a cage,—
   Sleep, little baby!

IV. *The Pansy*

The pansy makes such weird grimaces,
And imitates all bestial faces—
But there's a thing it couldn't do,
And that is, make a face like you.
I'm sure I've never seen another,
And that you got it from your mother.

V. *Lullaby*

Hush, my darling, that infernal
Racket; dearest, do!
Mamma is not all maternal—
She's a woman too.
Papa may of mamma tire;
He's been wed too long;

But the others who admire
Cannot all be wrong.
   Sleep! Sleep!

Men must work, and so they should, dear,
Lest their women weep;
Drawing water, hewing wood, dear,
Helps them go to sleep.
But your mamma sleeps in daytime,
When the sparrows twit,
And when night is here, her playtime,
Mamma wants to flit.
   Sleep! Sleep!

Now I hear the jazzu calling,
Calling to its own—
And if you don't stop your bawling,
You will bawl alone.
Yes, my lambkin, I adore you;
Mamma's kind and true;
But never think because I bore you,
You can bore me too!
   Sleep! Sleep!

VI. *The Tree*

See the leaves upon the tree!
That is where they ought to be:
Whether they be foul or fair,
Papa did not put them there.

VII. *The Doll*

Here is the little doll I brought you—
It shows the kind of simp I thought you!

VIII. *The Bird*

I love to hear the little bird
Into song by morning stirred,
Provided that he doesn't sing
Before my own awakening.
A bird that wakes a fellow up,
Should have been a buttercup.

IX. A *Father's Heart Is Touched*

When I think of all you've got
Coming to you, little tot:
The disappointments and diseases,
The rosebud hopes that blow to cheeses,
The pains, the aches, the blows, the kicks,
The jobs, the women, and the bricks,
I'm almost glad to see you such
An idiot, they won't hurt you much.

X. *Lullaby*

Sleep, my little baby, sleep;
You'll have cause enough to weep—
Slumber is a precious boon;
You'll be getting measles soon;
Mumps will claim you for their own;

Croup will change your infant tone.
Sleep, my little darling, sleep,
Ere your first bicuspids peep
Through your rosy little gums,
And the envious colic comes.
Oh, the troubles Time will ladle
On your happy baby cradle
Very shortly from the deep!—
So, be wise, my lamb, and sleep.

XI. *Zoology*

The elephant's a ghastly beast
That haunts the countries of the East;
The hippopotamus, I think,
Never gets enough to drink;
At any rate, I hear the dub
Never leaves his muddy tub;
The eagle dwells upon the steep
And feeds on savages and sheep—
What's the good of having that
Awful rot beneath your hat?

XII. *To a Chubby Little Girl, Aged Three*

The jungle is a kind of grove
Where lions, apes and rajahs rove;
It's not the kind of place that I
Should choose to live in, or to die;
Yet I should just as soon be in it
As hear you blab another minute.

XIII. *The Wind in the Tree*

When the wind is in the tree,
It makes a noise just like the sea,
As if there were not noise enough
To bother one, without that stuff.

XIV. *The Calf, the Goat, the Little Lamb*

The calf, the goat, the little lamb,
How easy is their day!
They do not seem to give-a-damn
For anything but play.
Each hour its simple pleasure brings,
And not a thing to do,
And yet, like other living things,
They end up in a stew!
And so did I, my little lamb,
And so will you.

XV. *The Gnu*

The gnu is a remarka-bul,
From all descriptions, ani-mul;
Yet how remarka-bul must you
Appear to the eccentric gnu!—
I have no doubt that even I
Must puzzle his peculiar eye;
There's something wrong with all of us;—
Let's ask the hippopotamus.

XVI. *Papa Sings (And How!)*

The moon is made of Stilton cheese;
Polar bears can never freeze;
In summer there are lots of flies;
Pumpkins end in pumpkin pies;
Rivers flow into the sea;
You don't look a bit like me;
When it's winter, then it snows,—
Scoot! You've got your mother's nose!
Germans drink a lot of beer—
Now, you pest, get out o' here!

XVII. *Mamma Sings*

Go to sleep, my little oaf,
Mamma's darling sugar-loaf;
Go to sleep and stay that way
For at least a night and day;
I'm no angel up above—
Don't abuse my mother-love;
I can stand so much and then
Mamma wants maturer men.
Sleep, my little plague, sleep tight;
My complexes are bad tonight,
And papa's friend is waiting now
To add a horn to papa's brow—
So sleep, my onus, sleep my own,
For if you bawl, you bawl alone.

XVIII. *For Drum and Harmonica*

Sleep, my darling baby, sleep:
The French eat frogs; Australians, sheep.

Today will go, tomorrow come;
I'll bake a cake and give you some.

Angels through your slumber sing!
A kangaroo's a funny thing.

A kangaroo will make you laff,
But not so much as a giraffe—

Not so much as a giraffe;
I'll bake a cake and give you haff—

A chocolate cake and a gooseberry tart;
Sleep, my darling; have a heart!

Don't you worry; ma will keep—
You yelled all day and now you sleep!

XIX. *For Little Boys Destined for Big Business*

Sleep, my baby, little elf;
Grow up honest—with yourself!
Always unto others do
What they'd like to do to you.

Love your neighbor—he may be
Useful; and besides it's free;
But should he more than friendship seek,
Always turn the other cheek.

Help the needy—all that's lent
Brings from six to ten per cent;

Place your trust in Heaven, but keep
Your money working while you sleep.

Loyal be to loyal friends;
Make them pay you dividends;
Work, like the industrious bee,
Your friends and foes impartially.

While the tender conscience frets,
All things come to him who gets;
All that glitters will for gold
Glitter more a thousand-fold.

Plutocratic precious, sleep:
Finer feelings all will keep;
Easy lies the head that wears
A crown among both bulls and bears.

XX. *For Little Boys in General*

Hush, my darling; do not cry—
You'll have cause to, by and by;
Blonde or Titian or brunette,
Some of them will get you yet.

You'll grow up and then you'll fall—
You'll have reason then to bawl;
You'll be glad to get some sleep,
For men must work, or women weep.

Men must work, while women try
To want the things they have to buy,

45

And while they try so hard to want,
Men must labor and grow gaunt.

When I look at baby's brow,
How I hate the hussies now!
Mamma'd save you if she could—
Sleep now, while the sleeping's good!

XXI. *For Little Girls Only*

Rock-a-bye, baby; why do you smile?
Are you rehearsing how to beguile?
We'll mould your expression just the right way:
Your natural look is a bit too blasé.

Mamma will tuck her little one in;
Sleep now, my darling, it's good for the skin;
And skin is important, for soon comes the day
When baby commences her skin game to play.

Mamma will help you, mamma advise,
Take the hard look away from your eyes;
Mamma will tell her lamb what to do,
Then Ziegfeld will come and glorify you.

Panacea

~~~~~~

I chant the homely bard who sings
The solace of insentient things;
Who lays upon his gall and grief
Balsamic bush and unguent leaf;
Who slips his humors to the hill,
His dolors to the daffodil.
I've taken many a desperate chance
With seventy kinds of shrubs and plants;
Consigned my toothache to the trees,
My heartbreak to the Pleiades.
The red and therapeutic rose
Has healed me of corrosive woes,
And much I owe of health and ease
To blooming beets and peonies.
When trouble smote me, zip and thigh,
I've winked at the narcotic sky;
I've taken creditors to stare
Upon the liquidating air,
And soothed the bloodhounds in their breast
With, "See the sun sink in the West!"
I've clipped misfortune's panther paw
With natural phenomena,
And poulticed worry and disease
With Christian Science cabbages.
Oh, let the years their sorrows yield—
The brook is gurgling through the field;

The high and homœopathic stars
Will heal my wounds and leave no scars;
The rainbow hurdle miles and miles
Of zooming Fords and cloudy stiles,
To lay upon my fear and fret
Her cool and glowing amulet,
While panaceas straight from God
Leap up in lilies from the sod.

Oh, hail, the homely bard who sings
The solace of insentient things:
The sky, the sea, the air, the ground,
Where perfect lenitives abound!

*Songs About Life and Brighter Things Yet;
A Survey of the Entire Earthly Panorama,
Animal, Vegetable and Mineral, with Appro-
priate Comment by the Author, of a Philosophic, Whimsical, Humorous or Poetic Nature
—a Truly Remarkable Undertaking*

I

Nothing from a straight line swerves
So sharply as a woman's curves,
And, having swerved, no might or main
Can ever put her straight again.

II

Men in single state should tarry;
While women, I suggest, should marry.

III

Some folks I know are always worried,
That when they die, they will be buried;
And some I know are quite elated
Because they're going to be cremated.

IV

Oh, it is cruel and inhuman
Not to pick up a fallen woman!—

The man who will not pick her up,
Shall have but water in his cup.

V

Where primal instincts do not slumber,
One sex the other does outnumber:
Men, e.g., are scarce in Paris—
The cause of which, *on dit*, the war is—
And the status that prevails
In London is a dearth of males;
While twenty fellows in Manhattan
Jump for the chair that Jenny sat in.
'Tis bad, I think to have too many
Women around a man—if any.

VI

A queen as torrid as Sumatra
Was the famous Cleopatra,
While Queen Elizabeth, I gather,
Contained herself in hottest weather:—
Proving that even queens can vary,
(And how!) like simple Madge or Mary;—
Yet spell them with an a or e,
They look a lot alike to me.

VII

It must be terrible to be
The kind of man they call a "he";
A man who'd rather fight than eat,
And doesn't have to cook his meat;
To whom a million women cling;
Who's not afraid of anything;

Who aims with an unerring eye
When circumstances justify;
Whose breadth and brawn and strength
      and size
Demand continual exercise;
Who rises every day at five
And feels it's good to be alive;
Who burns up leagues of windy plains
While weaklings wilt in subway trains.
Personally, I prefer
To be a guy who hates to stir;
Who stares with moist, suspicious brow
For signs of malice in a cow;
Who couldn't climb upon a horse
With pulleys, ladder, threats or force;
Who hasn't brains enough to care
About the foulness of the air,
And doesn't know that oxygen
Is breathed by all red-blooded men
The wide world over, east and west,
And sprouts in hair upon the chest;—
A fish, who lets his vigor lapse,
In dusty towns, where men are saps;
Who every manly art abhors,
And moulders in the Great Indoors.

Although a man like that disgraces
His brothers of the Open Spaces;
Although his chest is bald and flat,
There's something underneath the hat
Of such a man—a kind of demon
That lets him boss ten thousand he-men,

Who gallop grandly o'er the plains
And bring him home their hard-earned gains;
And though he's anything but strong,
He lives as healthy twice as long.

VIII

I'd rather listen to a flute
In Gotham, than a band in Butte.

IX

The serpent has no feet or hands,
Yet makes his way in many lands;
But who would on his belly crawl
In order to avoid a fall?

X

The leopard cannot change his spots:
In short, they're his forget-me-nots.

XI

Sometimes, in the dead of night,
Beyond the tiger-yellow light,
I hear the silence; then I see
It sprawling cat-wise comfortably,
With high back arched against the skies,
And starry languor in its eyes,
Transparent in transparent air,
Yet darkly outlined to my stare.
Then it occurs to me if that
Content and immemorial cat

Moved its ubiquitous, soft paws,
And opened those impalpable jaws
And spoke—what revelation then
Would flash and thunder upon men;
What light apocalyptic would
Shine from the eyes of evil and good;
What speech articulate would fall
From stars in the air's confessional;
What secrets joy and woe would sing,
And the stone mouth of Everything!

Then it occurs to me, as now,
That all that cats can say is "*Meow!*"

XII

Stars reflected in the water
Are jewels enough for Pharaoh's daughter;
But Pharaoh's daughter's dead and gone
While living girls are getting on.

XIII

The oyster never leaves his shell,
And does, therein, exceeding well;
He does not have to sweat and brood
To know the joys of oysterhood;
He deems the treasured pearl a fault,
And takes his world with ample salt.

XIV

From coast to coast the railroads roam,
Yet every inch of rail stays home.

XV

Twinkle, twinkle, little star,
But stay, my darling, where you are;
Into my life if you should fall,
I'd never see you shine at all.

XVI

There's no one that I'd like to be
One half so much as I or me,
And though I sup on meager bran,
I'd change the menu, not the man.

XVII

They say a rolling stone's a loss:
And yet I see no use in moss;
I'd rather gypsy through Cockaigne
Than vegetate a dubious gain.

XVIII

There are strange creatures in the zoo,
Like emu, zebra, auk and gnu,
But stranger creatures have I seen
Riding in a limousine.

XIX

It drinks up all—and yet the sea
Exceeds not its capacity;
Alas, how much a man must fret
To keep himself as strong—and wet!

XX

Blossoms in a May-day breeze
Are like lovely promises;
They delicately seem to say
That every bud will have its day,
Will blossom, ripen and be fruit,
And very often, canned, to boot!

XXI

The church, for all its Heavenly birth,
Can never leave the lowly earth,
While I, of more profane extraction,
May walk myself into a fraction;
May scale the air, the sky explore,
And knock at Heaven's very door;
Which shows that I have more a mind
For Heaven, than any church you'll find,
And that the spire, which Heavenward points,
Is still with Heaven out of joints.

XXII

I do respect that noble man
Who, when he's full of trouble can
Preserve a bright and cheerful mien
As if his life were all serene;
But I prefer the fellow, who
Is lively as a kangaroo
And beams and shouts with pure delight
When everything is going right.

XXIII

The ostrich lives in foreign lands
And trots along the burning sands,
And when from foes it would escape,
It hides its head—the silly ape!

XXIV

There's nothing sweeter than a bride
If you're not standing by her side;
But if you are, I learned in books,
You'll never see how sweet she looks.

XXV

The rose is so improvident
It never saves a single scent,
Without which fault, you must agree,
The rose would smell like you or me:—
Alas, that vices often are
The virtues of a flower or star,
Which paints the night upon the deep,
While men and swine are fast asleep.

XXVI

There's nothing that I have to say,
You haven't heard a duller day.

XXVII

The camel has a hump, but he
Looks just as curiously at me.

XXVIII

The tailor sews and gets the pip;
The tailor sews while others rip.

XXIX

The parrot does the best he can
To imitate the talk of Man,
But since he has no gift for speech,
The best the bird can do is screech.

XXX

See the serpent in the grass!
Stand aside, there; let him pass!
Oh, how happy he could be
With the smallest leg-acy!

XXXI

The dinosaur and icthyosaur
Are not among the things that are,
Though once the beasts were features;
Ah, sad it is to contemplate
How Nature can eliminate
Unnecessary creatures!
Perhaps she will, at last, extend
The process to another end—
To man, and even woman,
And turn the final hose of Fate
And give the biologic gate
To the obnoxious human!

XXXII

How doth the busy little bee
Improve each shining hour? Well, how?
The shining hour, it seems to me,
Still wears no honey on its brow,
Nor is, for all that I can see,
Improved by man or beast or bee.

XXXIII

The apple grows so bright and high,
And ends its days in apple pie.

XXXIV

When I was young, my hopes ran high—
My hopes did run, and so could I;
They danced upon the mountain tops
Oblivious of the traffic cops;
They swung, like monkeys in the trees,
From sun and moon and Pleiades;
They frolicked on the farthest wave
And thumbed their noses at the grave;
They thumbed their haughty bugles long
At men and creeds and right and wrong,
And gave the tin-horn days to come
Their only sound of fife and drum:—
Well, now my thyroid youth is done,
I'm very glad my *hopes* had fun!

XXXV

The ant, he lays aside some dough
Against the time of cold and snow;

He doesn't trust a bit to luck,
But gathers his assorted truck:—
If I could live just like the ant
I'd be as thrifty—but I can't.

XXXVI

The monkey chatters in the tree
Without a point, incessantly,
And thence bequeaths to Man his looks,
His conversation and his books.

XXXVII

The pansy is so slight a flower,
You'd think it could but live an hour—
So fragile is its grace;
And yet the little thing can dare
The lion's countenance to wear
Upon its pretty face.

How often does the meanest thing
Bestrut its fancy like a king
And walk a royal way!
For every wolf in sheep's attire,
A hundred thousand sheep aspire
To stalk the helpless prey.

XXXVIII

Content with things in miniature,
The humblest gold-fish is not poor;
His small aquarium is quite
Sufficient for his small delight;
He does not crave the flowing stream,

Or of the mighty ocean dream,
But with a little weed and gravel
Will simulate extensive travel.
A crystal dungeon cannot fret
Or chafe his spirit—if it's wet;
But he, with aqueous content,
Makes bright his mean environment:—
Glass walls do not a prison make
For fish who find a bowl a lake;
Who can, factitious weed beyond,
Behold the margin of a pond.

XXXIX

The farmer walks behind the plow
Which mops the ground as he his brow;
The sun, it broils the wretched man
Until the loam is not more tan;
The very horses seem to talk
About him, as before they walk,
Treading with ease their crumbly courses
And quite contented to be horses.
I know that I should rather be
A horse or cow or goat than he,
Which feed upon a natural hoard
Nor sweat and strain to keep a Ford.
A horse is placid, strong and clean,
It reads no Farmer's Magazine;
A barren stall, a simple oat
Are more important than its vote.
If I were on that hillside now
And that man's sweat were on my brow,
I'd fire a bullet at the sky,

Trample the lettuce down and die;
Or on a stream of salt self-pity
Float jocundly into the city,
Where, in the arms of that bright charmer,
I'd sing loud pæans to the farmer.

XL

Behold the graceful robin brood
On grass, in thoughtful solitude,
As if he meditated on
God's ways to robins, pro and con.
It seems that he must surely find
The seed of truth beneath the rind;
And yet I know the robin is
As stupid as his homely phiz,
And could no more evolve a thought
Than I, by whom this song was wrought.

XLI

The riveters across the street,
Like giant locusts in the heat,
With more than mortal malice rise
To hunt the Lion in the skies.
I know that all men try to shirk
A moiety of honest work,
Are liable to loaf or quit
Or oversleep or have a fit.
But riveters, before the night
Has packed its fardels for a flight,
Stand jocund on the girders red,
Like morning on the mountain's head.
If I but knew them, I should sing

The cryptic joys of riveting,
That calls its devotees from sleep
As prompt as tides upon the deep.
Meantime, in midst of all their ruction,
I hope they topple to destruction.

XLII

Now the mountain top is won,
Behold the valley in the sun—
The gold and yellow farms that lie
Bare-bosomed to the courting sky;
The olive hills, the meadows green,
The towns that punctuate the scene;
The little spires that seem to cry
For leaves and blossoms to the sky,
So delicate, it seems the breeze
Must stir them like the willow trees.
Ah, happy vale, how sweet you are,
As I observe you from this car;
How pleasant here to sit and shirk
And know your dwellers are at work!

XLIII

The miner wears a hob-nailed boot;
His clothes and face are black as soot;
He is a most fantastic sight
Among the lilacs fresh and bright.

XLIV

A lot of good it does a guy
To know that June is in the sky;
That in the fields the happy kine

On grass and clover amply dine;
That laurel on the mountain grows,
And bees are feeding on the rose.
I am no cow and cannot eat
Grass and clover 'stead of meat;
I couldn't chew a rose if I
Were threatened by the Wrath on High.
There's nothing I can get with honey—
I'm not a bee; I need the money,
And this bright office where I earn it,
What rose or laurel wouldn't spurn it?
I must admit, a blessed boon
To me is this same month of June.

XLV

I have only a bicycle,
And you have a motor car;
But your wife's a regular icicle
And as blue as the bluest star.

I have only a room and a bath
And you have a swell chateau;
But you're a case for a psychopath
And an allopath or so.

I have only one suit, in sooth,
And you have a couple of score;
But you have only a part of a tooth
Where a whole tooth grew before.

I have little of skittles and gin
And you have scuttles of wine;

But your troubles from women to insulin
Are nothing compared to mine.

XLVI

Tomorrow comes, tomorrow goes;
The thorn intrudes upon the rose;
The bee improves the shining hour
By robbing the defenseless flower,
Affording Man a Heaven-sent
And holy, natural precedent;
The river cannot flow uphill,
And Jack, (he thinks) must have his Jill:—
So varied is the dazzling store,
As times goes on, of human lore,
Though men invent and dig and sweat,
Discover algebra and fret,
Embroider heaven with their hopes,
And stare at bugs through microscopes.
Our sum of truth poor Lilith reckoned,
When Adam stole to Eve, his second.

XLVII

Though Cæsar stop a bunghole now,
With no green myrtle on his brow,
Remember, ere you shake your head
So wisely, that friend Cæsar's dead.
He does not stop, with mind and shin
And heart and occiput and chin,
The kicks and cuffs the fates bestow
On all who linger here below.
I'm sure, his dust he would not barter
For any living bunghole-starter.

XLVIII

I seldom mean a single thing
I say, or (as the phrase goes) sing;
But if it sounds both bright and true,
I like to think I think I do.

XLIX

If winter comes, with snow and sleet,
And a minimum of heat,
Spring can be so far behind
That I chase it from my mind.

L

Hope that springs eternal in
The human breast, is fond of gin,
Or Scotch or beer or anything
Designed to help a hope to spring.

LI

The dawn, it is a lovely sight,
So tender-blue and timid white;
A flower upon the eastern steep,
That blossoms while I soundly sleep.
I am afraid to stir or wake,
Lest, with the shock, the dawn should break,
And so, I sleep through many an hour,
Rather than hurt so frail a flower.

LII

I like the country very much:
The trees, the grass, the birds and such;

The crickets chirping in the dark;
The glow-worms with their sudden spark;
I like the sturdy hills that rise
In gracious worship of the skies;
The grove, the field, the church-like wood,
The sweet, adventurous solitude.
I like to watch the cattle graze
Silent in the sunny days:
The cows, that waking seem to sleep;
The woolly and untroubled sheep,
So simple and so unaware
They seem to blend into the air.
And yet I should be quite cast down
To see the country come to town.
I like the country best for this;—
Because they put it where it is.

LIII

Of all the birds that sing and fly
Between the housetops and the sky,
The muddy sparrow, mean and small,
I like, by far, the best of all.

His lot approaches human life;
His days are full of fear and strife;
He takes the traffic as it comes,
And pounds the sullen pave for crumbs.

No bird has so unsure a span;
He fights the elements and Man;
And so harassed is all his day,
He has no time to sing or pray.

From tenement to tenement
He flees, too frail to get the rent,
And then, his checkered days to crown,
A checkered taxi runs him down.

I

I've certainly learned a lot;
I've clarified many confusions;
I know when it's cold or it's hot,
And facts, as distinct from illusions.

I'm properly cynical, too;
Sophisticate, thoroughly urban;
I know what to say and to do,
And what to keep under the turban.

I've listened to Clara and Jane
In many informative sessions,
And I'll never be troubled again
With trifles like dreams and suppressions.

I've a swanky contempt for the sticks,
From Calgary down to the Isthmus,
And I laugh when I think of the hicks
Who really believe there is Christmas.

I'm up on the masochist set;
I'm at home with the ultra-sadistic;
I've registered extrovert sweat
Keeping pace with the introvert mystic.

68

I'm as doggy as Vanity Fair
In matters of art and of breeding;
I know what the invert will wear,
And the seventeen sexes are reading.

I live, as the saying is, hard;
I'm a stickler for freedom in books,
For women who travel Cunard,
And cuckolds who take it *de luxe*.

I'm quite *en rapport* with the time;
I'm thoroughly up to the minute;
And—wait till I finish this rhyme—
A hell of a lot there is in it!

II

I cannot reside in New York;
The backwoods have won me completely,
Where the boys believe in the stork,
And the girls are silent discreetly.

I live in a house on a hill
Surrounded by spruces and maples,
Where the spirit may garner its fill
Of wholesome and natural staples.

The birds and the winds never cease
A pæan melodious as Mozart,
Proclaiming the pleasures of peace,
As compared with the pains of the Bozart.

There the reverend sanctities walk
With a lordly and Israelite carriage,
And they penalize people who talk
Of art and companionate marriage.

I'm as free as a bird in the air;
I'm as hale as a fish in the *aqua*,
And the only discomfort I bear
Is the minor complaint of Chautauqua.

I live with an orthodox Lord
In a kind of suburban Nirvana;
My *corpus* is sound as a Ford,
And my *mens* is refreshingly *sana*.

I am far from the *dernier cri*
In dining and writing and fashions,
And I follow the bird and the bee
In the ordered régime of my passions.

I'm opposed to the trend of the time,
To the febrile caprice of the minute;
And—wait till I finish this rhyme—
A hell of a lot there is in it!

III

I yodel a bachelor life;
I sing of the joys of the single;
I scoff at a man with a wife,
And laugh at the thought that they mingle.

I cavort and I dine as I please;
I pay court to the vine and to beauty;
I blow (when I'm flush) like a breeze
From acquisitive cutie to cutie.

I am free of the fear of the wed
(For the female's capricious in temper)
That, at last, the inviolate bed
Will enact the familiar *sic semper*.

I am free in my work and my play,
My speech and my dress and my habits;
There is none *ex cathedra* to say
My brightest remarks are like Babbitt's.

I never have need to compete
With the wiles of a popular mummer,
And, provided I'm fond of the heat,
I can stay in the city all summer.

I never am prey to the thought
That my manner of loving and living
Is less than the bozos who taught
The missus the pleasures of giving.

The whimsies I serve are my own,
Be they politics, peaches or ponies,
With never a critical groan
From a creature of different hormones.

I am absolute lord of my time;
I am master and mate of the minute;

71

And—wait till I finish this rhyme—
A hell of a lot there is in it!

IV

The benedict's lot I espouse,
And my arteries quiver with pity
For the scholar, the sailor, the souse
Alone in the maw of the city.

Wherever they read or they roam,
Their lore and their liquor are hollow—
The sedative honies of home
Allay not the fevers that follow.

I sit in my cozy retreat
Where all but the doorbell is quiet;
The fender takes care of my feet,
And the *frau* does the same for my diet.

She is lily and lotus and light;
She is amaranth, rose and nepenthe,
And our ingle is cozy and bright,
And we look like a picture by Genthe.

My neurotic and ready dismay
At the troubles that try me and trample,
She keeps quite completely at bay
By her beautiful Christian example.

My health is offensively rude;
My closet is gaudy with raiment,

And the fellows who usually sued,
Are floored with a regular payment.

My smoking and drinking are par;
Our evenings are fruitful and clannish;
I'm learning to play the guitar,
To walk with my head up, and Spanish.

I've a sense of the value of time,
And I've ordered my days to the minute;
And—wait till I finish this rhyme—
A hell of a lot there is in it!

V

I sing of the sensitive soul—
The poet and dreamer and mystic—
And *cano* the glamorous goal,
That shines in the spirit artistic.

The troubles of Tellus I flee;
The bubbles of Helicon follow;
The argentine scales of the sea
I strum on the harp of Apollo.

Through delicate ether I swank,
And leap on the back of the Lion;
The fresh little breezes I spank
With the beautiful belt of Orion.

The mufti of reason I shed,
The boots of the weary and doleful,

73

And in Denishawn draperies tread
A cosmos pre-Einstein and soulful.

With Triton I tumble in brine,
And converse with the vagabond sparrow;
Of the boughs of the cedar and pine
I whittle Diana an arrow.

I escape the miasma and mist
Of the sowers and reapers and mourners,
And fly to my luminous tryst
With angels on heavenly corners.

The is and the was are my meat,
And I guzzle the wine of the will be;
My purple psychoses repeat
The trance of the tremulous Trilby.

I depart from the beaches of Time
In a shallop as frail as the minute;
And—wait till I finish this rhyme—
A hell of a lot there is in it!

VI

With lilies and languors I'm done;
With lotus and beautiful letters;—
I chant of a place in the sun,
And a horse in the van of go-getters.

I tug (as they say) at the leash;
I sniff at the roses of piffle;

I'm finished for good with hasheesh,
The lute and the lyrical sniffle.

The procreant Charles M. Schwab
I laud, as the ancients the phallus,
Who tickles the ducts of the mob
With pride in the virtuous callous.

My waking is loud with Success;
My sleep is impatient and nervous:
I ride with the mighty *noblesse*,
And distribute the coppers of Service.

I am sick of the sixty Beyonds;
Art bores me with every new mania;
I want to be Something in bonds,
And kind to the Queen of Rumania.

I long to be making the grade
And stand with the Mellons and Morgans;
I want to be Genghis of trade,
And Khan of conservative organs.

I play with the bulls and the bears;
I'm the Bartlett of market quotations;
I am in on the private affairs
Of the principal borrowing nations.

I am quite *en rapport* with the *Times*;
I am thoroughly up to the minute;
And—now that I'm done with these rhymes—
A hell of a lot there is in it!

Oh, Lord, Who knowest the human heart,
(A thousand other things apart)
Whose constant purpose is the good
Of all the human brotherhood—
Look down (accept this humble rhyme)
And guard us in election-time!
Oh, let the people vote for Biggs,
And not for Jiggs, or Squiggs, or Riggs,
Or Kelly, Cohen, Bing or Brown,
Or Toohey, Thompson, Tubbs or Towne!
When sorrow has no more surprise,
And stars look down like Borgia's eyes;
When hope and hair and teeth are gone,
And trucks and I awake the dawn,
How good, in this abyss of care
To know that Biggs is in the chair!
We do so much, perforce, by rote,
And often know not how we vote;
We stumble through the dark below,
But Thou canst see what way we go—
Thy Castle on the Upper Rhine
Commands a prospect extra fine—
So lend Thy vision to our souls,
And leave it with us at the polls,
That we may see the name of Biggs,
And not of Jiggs, or Squiggs, or Riggs.

With Biggs elected, what are then
The ninety million plagues of men?
What wretch, who would not be content
With Biggs as Mayor or President?—
Whose heart would break at last, if Brown
Achieved the goal, or Tubbs or Towne.
This troubled world would be so bright
If people did but vote aright;
Would be so free of grief and sin
If only men like Biggs were in;
If men like Biggs were Coroner,
Or Alderman, or Treasurer.
So, Lord, Who missest not a chance
To make the world like Paris, France;
Whose constant purpose is the good
Of all the human brotherhood,
When next election comes to town
(The view is excellent) look down,
Erase the names of Squiggs and Jiggs
And cast a million votes for Biggs!

~~~~~~

I. *The Shropshire Lad's Cousin*

(An Even Gloomier Fellow Than His Celebrated
Relative)

1

When I was one and twenty,
My ills were in their prime,
With aches and pains aplenty,
And gout before my time;
I had the pyorrhea,
And fever turned me blue—
They said that I would be a
Dead man at twenty-two.

Now I am two and twenty,
The aches and pains I thought
Were miseries aplenty,
Compared to these, are naught;
And even these are bubbles,
That scarce can worry me,
When I regard the troubles
I'll have at twenty-three.

2

With rue my heart is laden
For many a lass I had,

78

For many a rouge-lipped maiden,
That's got a richer lad.

In rooms too small for leaping
Such lads as I are laid,
While richer boys are keeping
The girls that do not fade.

3

Comrade, never take a bath,
For you'll tread the selfsame path;
For you'll do the selfsame work,
Where the dust and cinders lurk.

Comrade, cast aside your hope
Of the benefits of soap:
Though you scrub the morn away,
You'll be soiled at close of day.

4

Along the street as I came by,
A cinder hit me in the eye;
When I went walking in the field,
I stepped upon a snake concealed;
When in the woods I took a stroll,
A she-bear nipped my arm off whole;
When I went swimming in the creek,
A porpoise bit me in the cheek;
And so it goes, from dawn to dusk;
There's never corn; there's only husk.

When, famished, I sit down to eat,
The cook has always burned the meat;
When I would rest my weary head,
A score of mice are in my bed;
When cheerful friends I do desire,
Their houses ever are on fire.
There's nothing good, there's only ill:
In winter, hot; in summer, chill;
And when my time is come to die,
There will not be a grave to buy.

5

When I go to the circus,
My heart is full of woe,
For thinking of the people
Who used to see the show,
And now are laid below.

They stood beneath the tent-cloth,
And heard the lion roar;
They saw the striped hyena
Revolve upon the floor;
And now they are no more.

I think of all the corpses
Worm-eaten in the shade;
I cannot chew my peanuts
Or drink my lemonade:
Good God, I am afraid!

I see the grave-worms feeding
Upon the tigers' tails;

I see the people quiet
As prisoners in jails,
Because they're dead as nails.

Then what's the good of watching
The horses and trapeze,
The big show and the little,
And the menageries?—
We're all a lot of fleas.

6

I had three friends in Gotham,
And one of them is dead,
And one of them has palsy
And cannot leave his bed.

And now I know the other
Will soon desert me too,
And end his days in Sing Sing,
For something he will do.

7

Northward wing the happy swallows
To their olden haunts again,
And the poison ivy follows,
And the quinsy and the rain.

Soon the lovers will be walking
In the raw, malicious air,
Through catarrhal noses talking
Slush no mortal man can bear.

"Terence, this is fearful rot,
Putting poison in the pot;
All your song is measles, mumps,
Cramps and colic and the dumps;
Terence, you are rather frayed—
Go and have your teeth X-rayed."

Go ahead, my lad, and talk,
While your legs are fit to walk;
While your hair is on your head:
You'll not talk when you are dead.
Scorn, at will, my gloomy stuff;
You'll regret it soon enough.
Wait a year or two, and see
What a sorry sight you'll be;
Your liver and your eyes will fail;
You'll be languishing in jail;
You'll be run over by a cart,
And get a lesion on your heart;
Stir not till I have my say:
The girl you love will run away,
But she'll not stay away for good
And leave you to your solitude;
To her lad she'll not be true—
She'll come back and marry you;
And the kind of life you'll lead
Will make your bones and marrow bleed.
Wait a minute, I'm not through
With the things in store for you:
All you'll get to eat will be

Lettuce, nuts and hominy;
This much, too, I can foretell:
You'll get ill and won't get well;
Neither will you die, my lad;
Worse for you, and that's but bad;
You'll not die of mortal ache:
They will hang you by mistake;
They'll discover it too late,
Which is just the usual fate.
So I sing this doleful song
Just to dull your sense of wrong.
When you've read my verses through,
Not a thing can make you blue;
You will be prepared for all
Fearful things that will befall.
Fare you well, lad; on your way:
You'll break a leg ere close of day.

II. *Mr. Vachel Lindsay Discovers Radio*

In nineteen hundred and twenty-two,
A son of Italy,
A short, swart son-of-a-gun from Italy
Broke right through—
Broke through the ether with a bang and a crash,
Broke through the ether with a flip and a flash;
Yes, he did,
Sure, he did,
Did!
Did!
Did!

Crashed into the ether and broke right through
From Kennebunkport to Kalamazoo;
From Kalamazoo to San Francisco;
Broke right through
And invented radio;
Crashed through the air
Like a zim-zam Zbysco,
From Kennebunkport to San Francisco;
Tied up Cohen and Shultz and Harrigan,
From Portland, Maine, to Portland, Oregon—
Tied them up in knots of air—
Hey, you, Marconi, are you there?
Bill Marconi,
Son of Italy
Say, you, Marconi, are you there?
I'll say you're there!
There,
There,
There!
Crashing through the air
Without any wire;
I'll say you're there
Like a prairie fire;
Radio,
Radio,
Radio,
Radio!
Right through space with a crash like Zbysco,
From Salem, Mass., to San Francisco!
Hey, there, Buffalo,
Get that soprano!
Hey, there, Idaho,

84

Get that piano!
Get Paderewski pounding the piano!

X Y Z
W J G
P Q D
Hey, Pennsylvania,
Do you know
That California
Had an inch of snow?
Oklahoma is cloudy and cool,
And they're putting on their rubbers
When they send their kids to school.
Did you hear about the drop
In Minnesota,
And the bumper crop
In South Dakota?—
The bumper, bumper, bumper crop!
Listen in,
You son of sin,
Amalgamated Indigo took another flop;
Flop,
Flop,
Flop!
The ships on the ocean
Beat a retreat;
They're scared to death;
They hold their breath;—
There's a commotion down on the Street;
The bulls and the bears, and the bears and the
      bulls,
Tear one another's hair by the hard handfuls;—

The bulls and the bears
Are at one another's throats;
The bulls and the bears
Get one another's goats!
Radio,
Radio,
Radio,
Radio!
Hey, there, Bill,
Marconi Bill,
Hold 'em still,
While the news is crashed,
While the news is hurled,
Right through the centre of the bloomin' world!

W O P
F T G—
Shoot the news from every station,
Let it flash through all the nation!
Spark on spark,
Spark on spark,
Fiery needlepoints in the dark;
A million, billion, trillion, quadrillion,
Sextillion needlepoints hitting their mark.
The panther in the jungle,
The ostrich on the sand,
Is listening in
On Sousa's band;
The yak in the zoo
Is saying to the gnu,
"What's on the radio,

86

Gnu, what's new?"
The otter says
To the simple seal,
"I otter get
An ottermobile;
I heard all the prices,
At the latest show;
I heard all the prices
On the rad-i-o."
The lion and the tiger
Are jazzing on the sand,
They're jazzing on the Niger
To a Broadway band;—
Hey, there, Mischa,
Tune up your fiddle;
The Sphinx is getting ready
To unravel her riddle;
It's radio, radio, everywhere,
To the lamb in the meadow
And the llama at prayer—
Radio, radio, everywhere.

In the days when messages
Went by pony—
Those were the slow days, westward-ho days,
Those were the watch-your-step-as-you-go days—
Who would have thought that a guy like Marconi,
Nothing but a Dago
From across the foam,
A bloomin' Roman
Out of Rome;

Yes, he is;
Sure, he is;
Your teacher will tell you if she knows her biz;
Your father and your mother,
The corner cop,
Your sister and your brother
Will tell you he's a Wop—
Who would have thought that a guy like that
Would have the radio under his hat?
Well, he did;
Sure, he did;—
What does it matter if it's Dago or it's Yid?
Whoever did is the Kandy Kid;—
Yes, he is;
Sure, he is;
What does it matter where he got his phiz?
Radio,
Radio,
Radio,
Radio!
There's a guy who knew his biz!
There's a boy
Who stirred up things;
Who plays a fiddle without any strings;
Who taught us how to fly
Without any wings.
Hats off to you, Bill;
Hats off, boy;
From Pekin, China,
To Peoria, Illinois.
Radio!
Radio!

X Y Z!
Skips over mountains
And scoops up the sea;—
Who would have thought that a guy like that
Had the radio under his hat?

III. *Miss Millay Says Something Too*

1

I want to drown in good-salt water,
I want my body to bump the pier;
Neptune is calling his wayward daughter,
Crying, "Edna, come over here!"

I hate the town and I hate the people;
I hate the dryness of floor and pave;
The spar of a ship is my tall church-steeple;
My soul is wet as the wettest wave.

I'm seven-eighths salt and I want to roister
Deep in the brine with the submarine;
I speak the speech of the whale and oyster;
I know the ways of the wild sardine.

I'm tired of standing still and staring
Across the sea with my heels in dust:
I want to live like the sober herring,
And die as pickled when die I must.

2

My neighbor is a goose girl
And tends her silly geese;

89

But I love a rakish earl
And hunt the golden fleece.

My neighbor lives on bread and milk
And shuts her door on show;
But I would rather fall in silk
Than rise in calico.

My neighbor goes to bed at eight
And never sees the moon;
But I never stir till late,
And go to bed at noon.

My neighbor, fearful of a fall,
Was wed before her prime;
But I never wed at all
And have a better time.

What do I care if people stare
Or care what people say?
The golden dogs I'm going to
Are handsome dogs and gay.

IV. *Mr. Yeats Wants a Pot of Gold,*
     All of a Sudden

Belovèd, had I a pot of gold
Out of the coffers of the West,
Or even half a pot of gold,
I would buy you a cloth to cover your chest,
A green cloth and a blue cloth,

Gold or silver or even both,
A broidered cloth and a new coat
Out of the wool of a woolly goat,
And out of the hide of the boar that mourns
By Cummen Strand for his stolen bristles,
And lives on hazel nuts and thistles,
And blows all night on his mouse-gray horns;
With buttons made of the curds of the foam
That shimmer like cheeses in the gloam,
Until Maeve's voice and Niamh's would call
Like bitter winds from the grave, and bawl
Because a cloth and a coat like that
Knocked everything that went before,
The cloths and the coats the proud queens wore,
Into the shape of a cocked hat;
Because such a cloth and such a coat
Were enough to waken a queen's goat.
Belovèd, let not your heart be sad;
You know, as I am an Irish man,
By the buckle of Kitty O'Houlihan,
You know I would buy you the cloth if I had,
Rose of the World, a pot of gold,
Or even half a pot of gold,
And if you were untrue to me then,
Heart, I would take it back again.

V. *Mr. Walter de la Mare Makes the Little
Ones Dizzy*

1

When winking stars at dusk peep through
Pin-holes in the tent of blue,

91

Nurse puts spectacles on nose
And points them out to Little Lou.

With sad distempers all awry,
She stares with a myopic eye,
And mumbles names of stars and spheres
As they were letters in the sky.

Orion, Great Bear, Dipper—she
Cons them with a cracked "Tee, hee!"
While wretched Little Lou must keep
Nose to the pane unwillingly.

While ants crawl up and down his back,
She ties him to the zodiac,
And feeds him his astronomy
With many a salty pinch or whack.

Hour by hour goes slowly past;
The stars, like measles, fade at last;
Nurse goes upstairs, but Little Lou
Is to the window frozen fast.

2

When the Great Captain Sun goes home
And calls his spearsmen from the dome,
Sheep-bells, cow-bells, goat-bells and ram-bells
Tinkle and jangle in the gloam.

Pastures that were pistachio green,
In the slate dusk can scarce be seen,

And now are empty, where but late
Quick goats, slow cows, dumb sheep have been

Then elves, that make the barn their house,
And in the bins and mangers browse,
Bob up and down in oats and hay
And bleat like sheep and moo like cows.

3

Speckled with glints of star and moonshine,
The house is dark and still as stone,
And Fido sleeps in the dogwood kennel
With forelegs over his mutton bone.

Then out of the walnut wood, the squirrels
Peep, with their bushy tails upreared,
And the oak on the wood's-edge stretches his
        branches,
And combs with his roots his mossy beard.

Then ninnies and oafs and hook-nosed zanies,
And rabbits bred in the realm of Wales,
Dance and scream in the frosty starlight,
Swinging the squirrels by the tails,

Till out of the wood, Grandfather Nightmare
Rides in a chariot of Stilton cheese,
And eats the ninnies, the oafs and zanies,
The rabbits, the oak and the walnut trees.

VI. *Mr. W. H. Davies Snares Nature in a Few Felicitous Stanzas*

1

A rainbow in the rainy sky
Makes rainy too, my rolling eye,
And I could wish, when up I look,
That rainbows were not placed so high;
    Then might I pluck one
    Lightly down,
    And wear it proudly
    Through the town,
That all might stop upon their way,
Observe the lovely sight and say:
    "Upon my word, upon my word,
    A cuckoo and a rainbow, Lord;
    A sight that may
    Not come our way
    Again till heaven with moss is floored:
    May never come
    This side the tomb."

2

In every daisy in the field
Full thirty morals are concealed,
And though but one of them be mine,
And I forget the twenty-nine,
Yet am I better off by far
Than rich men and their butlers are,
Who ever have of morals none,
While happy I at least have one.

94

As lightly the wet fields I walked
Three leagues from London's noisy crowd,
I saw two ducks and seven drakes
And heard a blackbird singing loud.

Two dozen cows, knee-deep in grass,
I saw, and twenty-seven goats,
And heard a hundred sparrows pour
Upon a bank ten thousand notes.

And, though I've seen the golden notes
That rich men pour in city banks,
And know the sparrow's note is "cheep,"
I lifted up my heart in thanks.

VII. *Edwin Arlington Robinson Gets at the Root of the Matter*

'Well, now," she said, "that we are met again
Upon familiar terms that yet contain
Enough restraint to make it interesting,
I want to ask you in a friendly way
If you knew Peter Perkins?"
                                            "And if so,"
I answered, hiding my perplexity,
"You surely mean what I infer you mean,
That Peter Perkins was a man I knew?"

She smiled that wan and wandering smile of hers,
A soft confusion of her clarity,

And with her little finger flicked away
A speck of gold from out her shining hair.
I knew she heard me though I was not sure,
And cracked my knuckles in a casual way.

"We might as well be somber now," she said,
"And start to psycho-analyze this man.
He had a soul a stranger could see through,
And yet he had a trifling way with him,
Opaque transparency. I think the phrase
Has just enough simplicity to be
Complex enough. Don't crack your knuckles, please,
For Peter Perkins did that very thing.
I don't know why, do you?"

                              I turned away;
I sensed the tragedy in all she said,
Yet could not say a word.

                    "I like to think,"
She wandered on, "that Peter Perkins might
Have been an altogether different man,
If God had made him so. But as it was,
He was but Peter Perkins to the town;
His wife was Mrs. Perkins, and his son
Was Peter Perkins, Junior. That's the way
The world was made and that's the way it will
Continue to the end, unless it's changed.
Yet Peter Perkins when his hour had struck
Lay down and died. What else was there to do?"

I shrugged my shoulders. She went up the stairs.
A storm was coming up; I could not find
My hat, and so I stayed and watched it come.

VIII. *Poor Mr. Heine Suffers Some Translations
and Gives Up*

1

Maiden with the cheeks of cherry,
Maiden with the eyes of blue,
Much I thought you loved me very,
Much I thought that I loved you.

Me, alas, you have forsaken;
Now you love another lad,
And I see I was mistaken,
Thinking that I would be sad.

2

I dreamed I stood in the forest,
And heard the singing birds;
As sweet as thine were their voices,
And as meaningless their words.

I listened and listened and listened,
And thought I heard you call
Something out of the treetops
That didn't matter at all.

3

You are simple as a daisy,
You are blushful as a rose,
And your little teeth are pebbles
Over which a streamlet flows.

Nothing innocent as you are
Ever under heaven did go,
Nothing, Fräulein, save your lover,
He who used to think you so.

I

The day I like the least is Sunday,
And after that, I don't like Monday,
And after that, I don't care whose day
Tuesday is—I don't like Tuesday,
And after that, let other men say,
"Pooh," and "Bah"—I don't like Wednesday,
And after that, my very worse day
Is—in short, I don't like Thursday,
And after that, my evil-eye day
Is—the fact's,—I don't like Friday,
And after that, I won't grow fatter, say,
Because they have a day called Saturday—
But the day I like the least is Sunday,
And after that, I don't like Monday,
And after that, I don't care whose day
Tuesday is, I don't like Tuesday,
And after that, etc. . . .

II

I do not like to be alone:
My solar plexus turns to stone;
And yet, I know of nothing worse'n
Living with another person;
I hate to be a bachelor,
And marriage likewise, I abhor:—

99

Emphatically I resent
The things that people don't invent.

III

The year is at the spring, and so
Things begin to spring and grow;
Trees afford a shade, e.g.,
For those who can afford a tree;
Robins chirp and roses flourish;
Esculent herbs begin to nourish;
Fields are rife with floral data,
Which cows and sheep consume, pro rata;
Nature, squiffed on pre-war May,
Simply throws the stuff away:—
Four out of five, as things are now,
Get pyorrhea, anyhow.

IV

Grant me, O Lord, no neater rhyme,
Nor use nor usufruct of pelf,
But just a thought, from time to time,
Of something other than myself!

Oh, let me think of bug or beef;
Of Bismarck or the Caspian Sea,
Of anything to get relief
From that confounded nuisance, me!

I know myself quite well by heart;
I know the business of my soul,
And I should very gladly part
From that pestiferous rigmarole.

Oh, let me think of Joan of Arc;
Of truffles, queens and kitchen-maids;
Of George the Fifth and Central Park;
Of cheese and Labor Day parades!

Oh, let me think of Lipton's tea;
Of Prester John and Pilsen beer,
Of any bloomin' thing but me,
And that eternal, *"Weh is mir!"*

V

Soldiers have to fight and swear
To win the stripes they proudly wear;
While zebras, most unfit for war,
Have stripes enough to fill a corps.
Such unequal distribution
Is part of Heaven's constitution.

VI

Between the wanting and the getting
We lose our hair and hope in fretting;
So, when we get, the thing we've gotten
Is, so to speak, less ripe than rotten.

VII

In the merry month of Spring
Streams awake and robins sing;
Grass grows green, and sap begins
To tickle trees about the shins;
Flowers bestar the lively fields,
And every cow her quota yields;
The air is soft and so are you;

101

The sky, and all who think, are blue:—
Now isn't this a silly thing
For any adult man to sing,
Who might, with hefty he-men, range
The pastures of the Stock Exchange?

VIII

Babies haven't any hair;
Old men's heads are just as bare;—
Between the cradle and the grave
Lies a haircut and a shave.

IX

I never see the long giraffe,
But that I am constrained to laff:
It seems he'd starve to death before
His food could reach his humidor;
Yet so ingenious is the Lord,
He makes me think of Henry Ford.

X

The small chameleon has the knack
Of turning blue or green or black,
And yet, whatever hue he don,
He stays a small cham-e-le-on.

XI

A forest takes from every tree
Its individuality;—
There are so many in a wood,
None gets the courtesy it should;

While on the town's too barren page
A sapling is a personage:
A tree is wise to emigrate
To town, where it can stand in state.

XII

The brook comes tumbling down the hill
With H_2O the stream to fill;
The stream, it hurries all aquiver
With water for the richer river,
Which, in its turn, eternally
Runs with oblations to the sea;
But when the sea steams up in rain,
They get their water back again:—
None flies to serve another's ends
Without a thought of dividends.

XIII

The turnip and the cabbage are
Not lovely as a rose or star;
The beet and radish in the stilly
Earth, compare not with the lily;
A cow or sheep is not to be
Considered with a peony;
And yet, they brew delicious juices,
That have their sound plebeian uses;
Sans which, we'd all turn up our toes
At lily, peony or rose:—
Alas, that Beauty's thousand graces
Depend on Nature's homely phases!

103

XIV

The lapidary care bestowed
By God in fashioning the toad;
The expert craftsmanship which He
Spent on the gnu's topography;
The thought which loosened from that Brow
The crab, the camel and the cow,
With equal lavishness He spent
On many a priest and president.

XV

The horse, on his ferruginous feet,
Stands patient in the muggy street,
Untied, unguarded, and so free
To make a dash for liberty;
And yet, he stands and knows no goad
To shake his servitude and load,
And waits and bears the heat because
No rein is tugging at his jaws.
I watch the little men who pass
That dumb and dinosauric mass,
Whom he might, with a casual hoof,
Consign to the domain called "Pouf!"
And feel in every line and limb
Contemptuous of the likes of him.

XVI

The head that wears a crown may be
Inclined to some anxiety,
But, on the other hand, I know
A derby domes its meed of woe;

The straw, Fedora and the plug
Top many a lined and harried mug!
The kind of lid a man may wear
Is not an index of his care,
And so, I'd rather take a sling
From Fortune kellied like a king.

Anthropological Note

When the mountains rose from fire,
And the seas fell down between,
Ere the rock confessed desire
In a bacchanal of green;
When Earth sizzled like a sun,
And the steaming tempest raved,
There was none to sin, and none
To be damned or to be saved.

In that time the Lord could look
From His heavenly balcony
On a land no sages shook,
On a free and fishless sea;
There was neither beast nor bird
To disturb His quiet days;
None to slay Him with a word,
None to damn Him or to praise.

But a mischief in the blood
Even of a God is rife,
So He took a bit of mud
And He tickled it to life;
Deemed it just, perhaps, a jape;
Had no calculated plan—
But the mud became an ape,
And the ape became a Man.

Well, it proved a sorry jape,
And His troubles then began,—
For the mud stayed in the ape,
And the ape lived in the Man;
And the mud the ape perplexed,
And the ape the Man did prod,
And the Man, in his turn, vexed
With his irritations, God.

This the Lord had not foreseen;
This was never in His plan;
And it roused His holy spleen,
So He turned at last on Man;
And they've dealt each other blows
Since an immemorial day,
Till the Man is drunk with woes,
And I'm sure the Lord is gray.

Though they sometimes call a truce,
And a friendliness pretend,
I can hear His, "What's the use!
It is time to make an end."
I can see Him in His ire,
In a super-Freudian dream,
Throw the hills into the fire,
And the Man into the steam.

Interlude, for a Solitary Flute

I

Little I knew, when morning-white
Mated merrily with the green,
How rare a thing, how very rare
Was true despair!

Though I made songs of dark delight
Of things I had not felt or seen,
Little I knew how rare a thing
Was this despair I used to sing!

Now morning-white and leaf-green
Have quarreled, and seldom kiss or speak,
I know how rare, how far from fair
Is true despair!

Much have I felt and much have seen,
And now I know a life may break
As a twig is broken from a tree—
God pity all our company,
If God there be!

*For now I know how rare a thing
Is this despair I used to sing!*

Let those who can, cling close to God,
Against the day when this may be:
Ibis or priest or fane or fire,
Totem or tomb or creed or choir;

Seize Him in sky or sea or sod,
Temple or hill or scroll or tree:
There is no other song will bear
So dread a burden as despair!

Cling close to Him, forlorn Man;
Cling close to Him in bog or spire:
There is no other song will bear
So still a burden as despair!

*For now I know how rare a thing
Is this despair I used to sing!*

Sing it, sing it, if you can;
String for the song a lesser lyre,
And see how suddenly the note
Dies on the steel in brain and throat!

*I know how rare, how rare a thing
Is this despair
I used to sing!*

II

Some shall dig
The hills of Use,
And some shall follow
The Gold Wild Goose.

And the hills shall open
And be revealed,
And their glittering fruits
The rocks shall yield—

Thrones and chariots
For lords of Use,
And death for the hunters
Of the Gold Wild Goose—

The Gold Wild Goose
That cries in the mist
With the voice of Buddha,
The voice of Christ,

The voice of Mohammed,
And Moses' voice,
Till they who hear it
Rise and rejoice—

Rise and follow
By land and sea
To Mecca or Ganges
Or Galilee,

And die in the desert,
Or die in the stream,
Or die on the hill-top
Dreaming a dream

Of the Gold Wild Goose
That cries in the mist

With the voice of Buddha
Or Moses or Christ.

III

Sorrow that cries
Like a wind on water,
Is still of Eve
A natural daughter.

For a man may lie
With her, and she
Will give herself unto him
Utterly.

For Sorrow's a woman
A Man may take
And know, till his heart
And body break.

Sorrow, that cries
Like the windy waters,
May bear him sons,
And bear him daughters:

Heirs of substance,
And heirs of breath—
Hope and Dream,
And even Death;

Power and Tears,
And Prayer and Faith,

Strength and Song—
And even Death.

But Joy is a sylph
In the winter air,
That cracks his name
With the whips of her hair.

For a man may lie
With her, and she
Elude and flee him
Utterly:—

Body to body,
A hell apart,
With her laugh in his brain
And her loss in his heart.

And she will bear him
This bastard twain—
The monster, Fear,
And the hunchback, Pain.

A man may lie
With her, and she
Leave in his arms
The salt of the sea;

A knife in his heart,
And drouth on his breath,
Terror and Pain—
But never, Death.

But Sorrow, that cries
Like a wind on water,
Is still of Eve
A natural daughter.

For a man may lie
With her, and she
Will give herself unto him
Utterly,

Till the sun's red thunder,
The night's black drum
Cease, and his love
His peace become.

IV

We took our love by each white hand
And went into a summer land,
Where fadeless fruit and blossoms blew,
And amaranth and lotus grew.

And there the flower of sleep we ate,
And bared the breast of our dreams to fate,
And when the veins of the moon ran white,
We drank the ichor in leaves of night.

And yet we knew, we knew it well,
That love must tread the asphodel;
That noon would conquer with drums and brass
The honied silence of love and grass.

113

The hours that fell at our feet we threw
Like fretful pebbles into the blue,
And when the eyes of our love looked far,
We screened his dream with the morning-star.

When sundown sang of a day that's dead,
We twined the amaranth round love's head;
We laughed our thought of the singing free,
And lifted love for the sun to see.

And yet we knew, we knew it well,
That love must walk on the asphodel;
That time would conquer with steel and brass
The pitiful heaven of all who pass.

V

Behold the crowd; from far it seems
Such horror as an insect dreams;
A swarm of super-bugs that prey
On lesser beetles night and day.

How monstrous must the mass appear
To wretched flies abuzz with fear!
And what tremendous fireflies
The linkèd glitter of their eyes!

And they, in their turn, how they must
Ant-wise speck the crawling dust
To the calm, observant Eyes
Whose roomy sockets are the skies!

How furtive from its spacious place
Peers that still, derisive Face!
How human is the impulse that
Brings that mighty Palm down flat!

They tread the ant and crush the fly,
And soar a handsbreadth toward the sky,
And light, in their fantastic pride,
Into the Lord's insecticide.

VI

In the fine land of Nowhere,
On the far side of There,
We shall be very happy,
We shall have no care;
You will be the blossom;
I shall be the bough;
In the great time coming
After Now.

While you are crying,
Listen to my song;
My own heart is breaking,
But I shall be strong:
I shall be strong for thinking
Of the fine days and fair,
When we are done with being
Anywhere.

While you are grieving,
Listen to my tune:

I shall be the heavens,
You will be the moon;
You will be the breezes;
I shall be the air;
When we are done with weeping
Everywhere.

Sorrow shall not know us,
Though we be her tears;
Time shall not trouble us,
Though we be as her years;
For we shall be the silence
That sits behind the door,
In the long time coming
Evermore.

VII

No tree where lunar angels light,
No birds whose feathers are afire,
No hallelujahs in the night,
When stars and silence are the choir.

No apparitions in the dawn,
No sprite mercurial in the moon;
The vision and the music gone,
That were the first and only boon.

Only the ground with stones and worms,
Only the road that's hard and long,
Only the twisted human forms
Whose labor is their only song.

Only the hour of troubled dust,
The brambled bower, the windy ways;
And shall I say, "Come, share my crust,
Come share my cruse of stagnant days—

"My love, whose wandering eyes still sail
Like ships upon the burning west;
For whom the enchanted nightingale
Sings Latmos up within your breast"?

And shall I say, "Let Latmos be:
Endymion wanders, lost and blind,
The endless night of Thessaly
Whose nightingale is but a wind"?

My love, tall ships with chiselled prows
Still sail where Triton shields his eyes,
And silver under silver boughs,
Endymion waits the moon to rise.

My love, for you the knightly years
Stand golden in the sundown's fire;
For you the hills uncross their spears
And bid you pass to your desire.

And shall I say, "Come, pause with me,
Whose springs are weary of their seed"?
And shall I so unfaithful be
To your dear love for my drear need?

Your mantle of blue waters don;
The lands with festival are rife;

117

Your shoes of loveliness put on,
And go, my love, and welcome life.

VIII

Share with the heavens, the wind, a star, a tree,
Your swift adventures into ecstasy;
But let your heart your lachrymary be;

Share joy with sunset and the craggy sea;
But let your heart your lachrymary be,
Then you shall walk with Love and Beauty free.

Give delicate Love your sweetest dreams for gain,
And make the Lord with your contentment vain,
But let your tears fall deep into your brain:—

Then, though the cancer eat your soul away,
Your malice shall be equal to the day,
And your sardonic strength the night dismay.

IX

The dream of that high roadway out of life,
Soaring above
The dust, the rending bitterness, the strife—
That men call Love,
I followed:
Blesséd be God, Who hung so bright a star
Above an abattoir!

The dream that shines upon the dying breath,
The desperate story
Wherewith men seek to light the mood of Death—

The dream of Glory,
I followed:
Blesséd be God, Who hung so bright a star
Above an abattoir!

The dream of Joy, the dream, that even Christ
Wrung, earth-accursed,
From the tenacious thorn, the thunderous mist,
The acid thirst,
I followed:
Blesséd be God, Who hung so bright a star
Above an abattoir!

The dream of Peace, where like a little wind
To the indifferent grass,
Life sings to the green quiet of the mind
Of airy things that pass,
I followed:
Blesséd be God, Who hung so white a star
Above an abattoir!

Blesséd be God, Who used me for this part:
Who, for the richer savor of His wine,
Crushed out of me the marrow and the heart,
The hope, the dream, and for an anodyne,
Hung star on lying star
Above His abattoir;
Blesséd be He, Whom men have wisely feared,
To whom the seas have sent their terror up—
And may there be no stain upon His beard
When next He quaffs the cup!

I

Now, alas, it is too late
To buy Manhattan real estate,
But when my father came to town,
He could have bought for fifty down,
And I should not be where I am:
Yet does my father give-a-damn,
Or ever say, "I'm sorry, boy,"
Or looking at me, murmur, "Oy"?
He does not grieve for what I've missed,
And yet I'm called an Anarchist!

II

I want to take a ship and go
Abroad, but where I do not know:
It isn't Paris, London, Rome,
Nagasaki, Naples, Nome,
Honolulu, Teheran,
Servia or Afghanistan;
And yet I want to take a ship
And give the place I'm in the slip—
Lord, tell me where I want to go;
Give a man a decent show!

III

I ought to go to church and share
With Him who sent it every care,
And yet I am, beyond belief,
Parsimonious with my grief,
While He, who sent me every sorrow,
Is far too proud to come and borrow.

IV

I count the wrinkles on my brow,
And wish I were a sheep or cow;
Better, by far, yield milk or wool
By carload and by bucketful,
And be allowed to stand and stare,
And nibble grass, and take the air,
Than dream of golden mountain-tops,
And be a mark for traffic-cops.
The cow, she neither writes nor reads,
But soundly sleeps and calmly feeds,
And takes the rainfall and the sun,
The profit and the loss, as one.
Love binds her in no bitter fetters:
She leaves her mating to her betters.
What though I swallow her at last?—
Her trivial cares, not *mine*, are past;
And should her mettle be in question,
'Tis I, not *she*, gets indigestion!

V

The green and leafy trees, they stand
A solemn and impressive band,

With decorations in their hats
Like admirals and diplomats;
And yet, their job is filling men
As dumb as they, with oxygen—
For all the splendid pomp they wear,
They do but pump the world with air,
Proving, that trees, beneath their hats,
Are admirals and diplomats.

VI

Of all the idiots that abound
Above, beneath, and on the ground.
The blinking squirrel is to me
The deepest-sunk in idiocy—
He builds himself a catacomb
Among the worms, and calls it home,
And there he cowers, sore afraid
Of bird and beast and man and maid,
And when, at last, he leaves his rut,
His goal is just another nut.

VII

For sheer urbanity, I deem
A cat deserving of the cream:—
He does not sit and contemplate
The various aspects of his fate,
Or the strange world that round him flits;—
When he sits down, he merely sits.
Behold, upon my verses he
Reposes with su-a-vity,
Preferring the surrounding night
To anything that I may write;

Thus proving, that who most rehearses,
Is not the ablest judge of verses.
No feline Jezebel may vex
His placid interludes with sex:—
His destined hour must come to him,
Nor can it fret his interim.
It does not gnaw him like a vice,
That other cats may catch more mice,
Or that some remnants of his fish
Or liver linger in the dish—
His appetite once gratified,
He'll slumber by temptation's side,
Too much philosopher to wake
For catnip, siren, milk or steak.
He has a greater use for sun
Than Cæsar or Napole-on,
Who garnered naught but sweat and heat
Where Thomas toasts his noble feet.
Not bound by custom or by tub,
Finding a use in "There's the rub!"
Oh, cat, I'd give all Gilead's balm,
To have your cat—aleptic calm!

VIII

I burned my candle at both ends,
And now have neither foes nor friends;
For all the lovely light begotten,
I'm paying now in feeling rotten.

IX

The lion with his kingly rage,
Animates his arid cage,

123

And to his cubicle so bare,
Imparts a fierce and jungle air;
Proving—however some may take it—
That life is what they let you make it.

X

It is not Beauty's fault that I
No longer listen or reply,
When in a thousand various tones,
She plays her drums and saxophones,
To call, with sensitive alarms,
My spirit to creative arms.

It is not Beauty's fault, I gaze
With mackerel eye upon her ways;
Her greens and seres and lights and shades,
Her bright tableaux and swift parades.

My spirit still would much endure
To be her slave and paramour;
To be a partner in her spring,
And share her winter sorrowing;
To spend her suns' unminted gold,
And race her winds through hot and cold,
Or toss the silver of her moons
On bars of her divine saloons.

Alas, her gifts no longer stir
Because my glands are through with her!

XI

With me my little world shall die,
My personal earth, peculiar sky,

My biased God and special sight
Of trees and men and day and night;—
A sudden, conscious gleam withdrawn
From that great glass which mirrors dawn;
Two tangible hands, that reach above,
To that fierce groping which is Love,
And lead him down their narrow way
To warmth and refuge for a day.

My eyes have helped bewildered spheres
A pace or two along the years,
And my reality has given
An hour of glory unto Heaven;
My thought has shot its impulses
Through ocean's mighty arteries;
And bits of disentangled mud
Have drained the scarlet of my blood;
Have stolen the quickness of my breath
To stand like roses, flaunting Death.

Oh, I have been a friend to bless
To all the host of nothingness;
Have shared my tiny store—and yet
How soon these ingrate things forget:
The earth, the sea, the rose, the sky,
They'll get themselves another guy!

XII

I understand that women are
As fickle as a gift cigar,
And, as for all that I can say,
It may be so (I've been away)

But, fickle as the fair may be,
They're constant as calamity,
Compared to a capricious cuss
Who sports the name of Morph-e-us.

He'll say, "Lie down—I'm standing near;
Go pound (in ancient Greek) your ear;
Go linger in the poppy-dells,
And polish up your aging cells:
Your thyroid looks a trifle blue;
Your joints are drinking up the dew;
Your outlook's wild, your credit's wan,
And trucks will soon distribute dawn—
So, go and tumble in the hay;
Tomorrow is a tougher day!"

Oh, many a time (and even oft)
My billion-buttoned clothes I've doffed,
And hopeful as a babe unborn,
Prepared to sleep through dawn and horn.
I've thought of streams and forests cool,
And perfect shots in Kelly pool;
Of pastures where Pavlowa sheep
Interpret deep and dreamless sleep;
I've counted sheep and lamb and ewe,
Till we were mingled in a stew,
And in a dark and fatal hour,
My brave arithmetic went sour.
I've thought of dark and restful shades,
And not so dark or restful maids,
Of trees and cabbages in rows,
And this and that and them and those,

126

Till three-inch skies across the way,
Grew lovely with an eight-hour day;—
And yet, for everything I tried,
You'd think the bloody Greek had died.

Oh, go and say that women are
As changeful as a bootleg bar;
As Heaven's intent—but do not dare
Their fickleness to this compare.
Oh, do not dare, for if you do,
I fear I shall agree with you.

Carol for the Day After Christmas

I burn a reverential rhyme
Unto the modest Muse of Crime,
Unsung, unhung (I mean with bays)
But generous to her devotees;—

Not indiscriminately kind;
No friend to the burglarious mind;
No dour divinity of jail—
But Crime on an Extensive Scale!

Dear Muse (for nobler numbers fit)
Of Those Who Get Away With It;
For whom the fiscal welkin rings
With praise of cabinets and kings;

In whose benign and fecund shade
The grapevine sacrifice is made
By Forward-Looking Men, who know
Your cabalistic So-and-So;

By Leaders of the State and Thought;
By Princes of the Never-Caught;
By Lords of Enterprises, sung
As Great Examples to the young:

Accept this bow (from me to you)
And teach the bard a trick or two,
And toss him an excessive bit
From Super-Rogue-and-Hypocrite!

No Mighty Statesman would I be,
Or Banker to Democracy;
No splendid Chairman of the Board,
And sit upon the whole damn gourd;—

But spill a little of the loot
In decent radius of my boot;—
Your teeming harvest festival
Has swag enough for one and all!

Love-songs, at Once Tender and Informative
—An Unusual Combination in Verses of This
Character

I

Satyrs used to fall for nymphs,
Just the same as other symphs;
Same as many a modern goof,
Cupid kept them on the hoof.

II

A woman, like the touted Sphinx,
Sits, and God knows what she thinks;
Hard-boiled men, who never fall,
Say she doesn't think at all.

III

Breathes there a man with hide so tough
Who says two sexes aren't enough?

IV

I could not love thee, dear, so much,
Were I not born to be in Dutch.

V

Maid of Gotham, ere we part,
Have a hospitable heart—

Since our own delights must end,
Introduce me to your friend.

VI

She gave me her heart—
Oh, the sweetness of it!
She gave me her hand—
The petiteness of it!

She gave me herself—
Oh, the wonder of it!
I gave her myself—
Oh, the blunder of it!

VII

Little bride, come over here,
Tell me where you'll be next year;
Quite unfearful of my doom,
I should like to know with whom.

VIII

If you love me, as I love you,
We'll both be friendly and untrue.

IX

When you are tired of me, and I
Look mournfully upon the sky,
We shall be friends, I hope, and meet
Sometimes, and talk how times were sweet
When we were sure no sword could sever
Two people born to love forever.

X

When you are old, and want to stay
Beside the hearth the livelong day,
Weaving with memorial grace
Your youth in linen or in lace—
Oh, what a picture you will be
Of Age's sweet serenity;
A symbol of a tranquil home
From which but fools like me would roam!

XI

Let us build a little house
With instalments, love and craft,
Fit for you, my precious mouse—
Garden fore and garden aft.

There we'll love and play (I hope)
Work, beget and dream (I trust)
Sweetly with such problems cope
As plague whatever stems of dust.

We shall have such rosy tryst;
Ours will be a blessed fate;
Love will daily grow (I wist)
So (D.G.) will real estate.

When the jealous powers above
Magic from our couplet steal,
We may then conclude our love
With a profitable deal.

132

XII

My sanguine and adventurous dear,
Whom long experience taught no fear,
I shall make a ballad of
The repetitions of your love.

Every time you love again,
Former lovers failed in vain:
Your ardor rises like the sun
On the last and only one.

You but tell the simple truth
Out of your perennial youth;
When I sing of you, I sing
A heart whose every month is spring.

Marvellous unto my sight
Your quasi-virginal delight;
But dearer, sweeter, rarer yet,
How you remember to forget.

Bless your heart, that phœnix-wise,
Can from its amorous ashes rise:
The years their disappointments waste
On a memory so chaste.

XIII

Your little hands,
Your little feet,
Your little mouth—
Oh, God, how sweet!

133

Your little nose,
Your little ears,
Your eyes, that shed
Such little tears!

Your little voice,
So soft and kind;
Your little soul,
Your little mind!

XIV

Love, you brought me everything;
I gave little—
But the beauty that I sing
May be brittle;—

May be brittle, and so might—
Now I've spoken!—
Have fallen on another's sight
And been broken!

XV

The honey of the Hybla bees
Is not so sweet as kissing you;
Nor autumn wind in dying trees
So wistful is as missing you.

And when you are not mine to kiss,
My every thought is haunting you;
And when your mouth is mine, I miss
The wistfulness of wanting you.

XVI

Here we are together,
You and I,
In the amber autumn weather,
Yet we sigh,
And are quiet, disenchanted
By the bliss
That convinced us that we wanted
Only this!

Yet is this a cause for weeping
After all?
Isn't this a time for keeping
Festival,
When the high gods make decision
And ordain
That poor Cupid have his vision
Back again?

XVII

The lady of my heart is one
Who has no peer beneath the sun;
But mortal truths have mortal sequels—
Beneath the moon I know her equals.

XVIII

Had we but parted at the start,
I'd cut some figure in your heart;
And though the lands between were wide,
You'd often see me at your side.

But having loved and stayed, my dear,
I'm always everywhere but here,
And, still more paradoxical,
You always see me not at all.

XIX

My mate, my friend, my love, my life,
My bosom's—as the phrase is—wife;
My comrade in the hour of woe—
An hour whose limits I don't know—
My star in darkness, solace, balm,
My prophylaxis, refuge, calm,
Companion of the million blights
That plague my liver, purse and lights;
My pleasant garden in the gloam,
My all—if you were ever home!

XX

When I took you for my own,
You stood 'mong women all alone;
When I let the magic go,
You stood with women in a row.

XXI

In your anger be not just,
Lest your anger turn to dust;
Anger will make easy yet
The bitter footfalls of regret.

XXII

Darling, mistress of my heart,
In gray or sunny weather,

None but a better man shall part
What God has joined together.

XXIII

Without you, love, I must contend
With longing that has never end;
With loneliness, against whose bars
The sun is shattered and the stars;
With silence deeper than the sea,
That drowns the very thoughts of me.

With you, my sweet, I must endure
The cross of all who hold unsure
The precious boon; must ever hear
The insistent monotone of Fear;
Must ever toward the zenith ache,
Abasing self, for your dear sake.

In those serene and potent eyes
Is there no kindly compromise?
Will they not grant me this release:
To see their light and still have peace,
And let the deeps behind them be
For sturdier fish the fatal sea?

Epilogue

Now that the little penny sword is sheathed,
The trifling tourney over, the verse dismounted,
And nothing but a useless half-hour slain,
I am reminded of a man who breathed
Into this selfsame spirit lies that counted
More than his truths or half-truths shall again.
Even the heartbreak in his joy was good;
Even the blindness of his thought was better
Than squint-eyed gazing at the stolid sun
And getting spots for his enquiring mood:—
What will you find, then, but the form and letter
Of things when the meticulous search is done?
And will you say the moon has not her eyes?
And will you say the trees have not their speech?
And will you call the sterile difference wise?
And will you, then, the dead subtraction teach,
And say to youth and those remembering youth,
These ashes are the one and only truth?
How now, professor? Be that as it may,
A hell of a lot it matters either way!

Year In, You're Out

To those, who month on weary month,
Heard me proclaiming more than one-th
The nine varieties of woe
(Oh, more!) designed for us below;
Who listened, looked and answered, "No";
To Edith, Sally, Marty, Kay;
To Boardman ("Mike"), T.R. and Gay,
Who listened, looked, and said, "Go rhyme!"
This book—
Tomorrow is a tougher time.

Invocation

Come, lovely Muse, desert for me
Your leafy hill, your crystal spring,
Your Heliconian company
Who taught the earlier Greek to sing.

Your laurel and your lute forsake,
Your parsley-field and pleasant wood,
Your votive rose, suburban brake
And all its antic brotherhood.

Abandon to their goats and sheep
The herdsmen in their whispering home,
Where Pindar woke from sunny sleep
To smack Boeotian honeycomb.

Your myrtle and your April loves,
Your amber days, whose temperate sun,
Wind-winnowed in the ordered groves,
Is to your body subtly spun,

Your lunar mead, your starry glade,
Your fragrant and nectarean night,
Your bird liquescent in the shade
That melts melodiously to light;

Your sail beyond the morning sands,
Where Sappho, wandering from the sea,
To Phaon stretches fluid hands,
Come, leave, oh, Muse, and live with me!

Come, live with me and we shall make
Delicious and immortal moan,
And the fantastic bootleg shake
Unto the ductile saxophone.

Come, live with me and be my love
In statutory Christian sin,
And we shall all the pleasures prove
Of two-room flats and moral gin.

And you shall be a modern maid,
And golf upon the Attic greens,
Bisexually unafraid,
And talk about your endocrines.

And we shall to the heavens advance,
And broadcast to the quaking dawn
The age that walks in Puritan pants
With just one crucial button gone.

And we shall sing of export trade,
And celebrate the fiscal year,
And revel in the basement shade
Until the lusty riveteer,

Winds high and clear his rural horn
And the official day begins,

And we shall usher in the morn
With bowls of shredded vitamins.

Oh, come, sweet Muse, and share with me
My kitchenette and telephone,
And all my complexes shall be
Your true and circumambient own.

And we shall pluck the dulcet strain
From ukulele and guitar,
And look on Ford and Hoover plain,
And meet the cousins of the Czar:

The countless cousins of the Czar,
Grand Duke or Duchess, every one,
As multitudinous as are
The spheres (who borrow from the sun).

And we shall tune the choriamb,
And with the taxi-horn compete,
To bull and bear and little lamb
Who play together in the Street.

And airships overhead shall roar
The hymnal of our happy state,
Based on the single standard, or
If you prefer, companionate.

And Progress shall with every flower
Of sweet Expense her ardor prove,
If you will leave your dated bower,
Delightful Muse, and be my love.

Lyric, to be Skipped by Those Who Do Not Care for This Sort of Thing

We have starved on bread and meat,
Thirsted long on bitter wine;
Let us now the locusts eat
And suck the wind for sprays of brine.

Birds will wing from west and east,
Stars fly low from north and south,
Beasts approach to share our feast,
Sands grow fertile with our drouth.

In the desert let us be
Baptists of the single thought,
Till the solitude and we
The final ecstasy have wrought.

He, who drank the vinegar,
Took the thundercloud for bread,
Saw, at last, the evening star
Brighten with the risen dead.

Come Weal, Come Woe, My Status Is Quo

I. *Inventory*

The tallest buildings ever known,
The radio and the vitaphone,
Unfortunately, do not affect
My status in the least respect.

The flights across the wet Atlantic,
However curious, bold and antic,
Unfortunately, do not affect
My status in the least respect.

The consultations of physicians
About my various weird conditions,
Unfortunately, did not affect
My status in the least respect.

A green and prophylactic diet,
Fresh air and exercise and quiet,
Unfortunately, do not affect
God's malice in the least respect.

Parliaments and Presidents,
The fiscal year's combined events,
Unfortunately, do not affect
My status in the least respect.

But Eve's experiments with alien pleasures,
And ignorance of safe and simple measures,
Unfortunately, still affect
My earthly status in every respect.

A Spirit risen from her Hour of Bliss,
That hounded Cain and Abel through Genesis,
Unfortunately, still affects
My earthly status in all respects.

And the unsleeping dead, who range
Tissues and cells and brain and blood,
Unalterable foes of Change,
And friends of the primordial mud,
Unfortunately, still affect
My earthly status in every respect.

II

Now I see clearly as they are
Sun and moon and sea and star,
Grass and tree and all my kind
Without distortion of my mind.
Time has quieted my rage
And freed my thought of peonage.
No more I serve with singing fire
The lying altars of desire,
Or dream the things of air and sod
A falcon on the wrist of God.
Two and two are merely four
And often less and never more,
And I, for all the world's advance,
An upright mammal wearing pants.

Let poets more romantic sing
The *double entendre* of the spring,
The flower of faith, the core of love—
I know the algebra thereof.
I weigh the facts and note the dross
And am, in short, a total loss!

III

How sweet upon the silent night
To meditate the hours in flight;
To dream upon the awful Plan
That wrought bacilli, beast and man:
To ponder the design above
That fashioned locusts, llamas, love,
The ocean's broad and iron track,
The zebra and the zodiac!
When I consider all that is,
I feel the wonder on my phiz;—
I feel my startled hair stand up
At thought of bee and buttercup,
The cow and her mechanic cud,
The circulation of the blood,
The senses, seasons, night and noon,
Zulus, women and the moon. . . .
Yet, swiftly as the minutes flit,
I realize I'm used to it!

IV

For hours and hours I could not sleep:
I counted horses, goats and sheep;
I heard the clock strike four and five,
And counted every beast alive—

Zebus, emus, yaks and gnus,
Enough for seventy-seven zoos;
Lions, tigers, droves and herds;
Serpents, insects, fishes, birds;—
A zoological survey
I made before the break of day,
And when there wasn't another sheep
Or bug to count, I fell asleep.

V

I've had troubles all my life:
Now 'twas storm and now 'twas strife;
Yet at honest trades I worked
Year in, you're out, and never shirked;
Then I married, settled down,
And kept on settling round the town—
(For, as you know, the life domestic
Is not always of the best-ic).
Did I grumble? Yes, I did,
But never had a thought to skid;—
"Honest toil," was still my motto,
"Is the way to get your auto"—
Though I knew that I could land it
As a bootlegger or bandit.
Well, some day, I'll have my fill:
The worm will turn—*but I'll lie still*.

VI

When I consider how we fret
About a woman or a debt,
And strive and strain and cark and cuss,
And work and want and sweat and fuss,

And then observe the monkey swing
A casual tail at everything,
I am inclined to think that he
Evolved from apes like you and me.

VII

The grass, it does not meditate
Upon its fairly low estate,
Or tell the laden wind that blows
Its envy of the richer rose.
When sun and drouth, that spare the oak,
Conspire to leave it flat and broke,
It does not hate the noble tree
For its impregnability,
Or worry how to borrow rain
From balmy Sicily or Spain.
It lets these trifles come to pass,
And just continues to be grass.
I wish, with just as little trouble,
I came to my eventual stubble!

VIII. *Tempora Mutantur*

Before Sir Isaac Newton sent
The Serpent back a riper apple;
Before Professor Einstein bent
The cosmos in a single grapple;

Before Marconi flung an S
Across the orthodox Atlantic,
And Freud confirmed our private guess
That sex was capriped and antic;

Before the Brothers Wright prevailed
On ether to endure the human;
Before the modest darkness paled,
When Man decided to illumine;

Before the very word Pasteur
Struck terror to the brute bacillus,
And Ehrlich left poor Venus poor,
With not a decent way to kill us;—

A man was born (as he is now—
The method shows no sign of failing).
He suffered from his fellows. (How?
Vide the manner still prevailing.)

He lost his teeth (as we do now,
For all Sangrado's dental capers),
And skilful fingers milked the cow;—
(*The others? Read the daily papers.*)

He groaned (like us) in care and debt—
Consult the archives of the breezes—
He earned his taxes in his sweat
And died (as we do) of diseases.

He dreamed in air and strove in dust
And bled for priests and politicians;
He learned to place his final trust
(Compare our own!) in the morticians.

He served a million gods (*what news!*)
With first his crimes and then his chorals;

He stole (*aha!*) his neighbor's shoes
And paid him back a set of morals.

In short, while scientists unborn
Prepare to search the stars and roses,
The snail is on his ancient thorn
And God in conference with Moses.

IX

Dear God, or Allah, Buddha, Christ,
Osiris, Zeus, or what You will,
Lord of impenetrable mist
And (what a range!) the daffodil—
Let not Your servant (me, of course)
Who, much as any man, admires
Your very tiniest *tour de force*,
Despise so much what he desires!

Let him (I pray You) either want
Completely, or be quite exempt;
Let him (a trifling boon) not haunt
The loud bazaars of his contempt,
Eventually there to find
The immemorial, dusty prizes,
And then, with a tormented mind,
Desire so much what he despises!

Grant me, I beg, if You have time,
A modest increment (unearned),
A fringe of unlaborious rhyme,
And leagues of sleep (my candle's burned);
A ton of *Sitzfleisch* for my mind,

151

Which noble longing often irks,
And for my solemn soul, the kind
Of grin that overspreads Your works.

Let me, in short, on Your estate
With You serenely rusticate!

The Stricken

Here in the static dark we lie,
My love, Insomnia, and I,
And hear (oh, Lord, again?) again
The brittle swish of blind rain
Groping with a mendicant sound
For the almshouse of the ground.

Here on the stony hour I lie
Rolling darkness from my eye
And stare like an unmoving sheep
At the pasture-line of sleep.

Oh, how the day's phenomena
Perplex my brain and viscera!
Ring, solemn dirge, in dour steeple,
Ring out Jehovah's dreadful terms!
The world is full of things and people;
The grave of worms.
Woe, woe, woe, woe!
And there's no other place to go.
Ring, ring, sour steeple!
Heaven is also full of people,
And hell is less a dire damnation
Than a literal translation.

153

On this brazier shall we heat
Our unreal and unutterable sweet?
On this clear and singing stream
Shall we drift into the dream?
We, who wonder
At the bottom of what water
Lies the stone of the dead thunder
And the wrack's wild daughter.

In the wood whose boles are blue
And high as the liquescent spheres,
That drench him with their fiery dew,
The immortal unicorn keeps tryst
With our far and faithless spears.
On this chariot shall we ride
To the passion in his side?
And how shall we be going soon?

In the dark chamber of the moon
Sits the Eternal Onanist,
Whose insane visions circle round
The breasts of the lascivious ground.
It is thus
Gnomic spirits enter us;
Salamanders burn our flesh;
Sylphs our simple wills enmesh;
Undines beat in us like waves
Crying for their phosphor-caves.
It is for this twisted birth
That we pay with death and fire;
Bodies to the bawdy earth,
Madness to our nubile Sire!

154

We are the toad's imagined spirit;
We are the tree-roots' animate fingers
Groping for the pitiful head
Of their particular dead;
The light that lingers
When the light is fled.
We are the sea-foam's birth-in-death;
We are the corpse's after-breath.
We are the ultra-violet
Of an anticipated regret.
We cannot see for seeing,
Or be, who are half-clothed in being.
We are the homesick
Born in the burning
Of our home.
Our root is a yearning,
Our roof is the gloom.
By back-stairs and by fire-escapes
We sneak to our enchanted shapes
Through nocturnes of the half-born, where
They moan between earth's loins and air.
We must die and die again
And eat the fire-hot heart of pain
To take our strange and baffled ease
In the apocalyptic land.

For there the candelabra stand
Whose flames are cold and white as snow,
And no shadow of them falls
On the penetrable walls
And the tall hush of tapestries.
We must go

From room to room and room to room
And pay especial tithes to Doom,
Ever, ever in arrears;
For we have broken and break the law;
We have opened the lion's jaw
And pitied the imprisoned years.

His head upon his fumbling paw,
We have seen the tiger's tears.

Couplets, Rare, Medium, and Well-Done

1. *The Ovum*

The tiny ovum does not know
Its own capacity for woe.

Oh, nor in bitterness nor in hate
Blame it for its developed state!

It prayed no aching prayer to be
The Son of God, or you or me.

Its hairless hide had little room
For fleas like *cogito* or *sum.*

Lay not to it your daily hurt:
Love came and did the creature dirt.

Who would have thought so small a chalice
Could interest His mighty malice?

It had no thought to injure us
When it beheld homunculus.

It fell, as women often do,
With never a thought of me or you.

157

And now, alas, it cannot quit
Unless you disensorcel it.

Oh, give the wretched creature gas
And it will gladly go to grass!

Oh, hang yourself and let it be
As innocent again and free!

One slip for love was never meant
To bring such dreadful punishment.

II. *Man*

The ways of other creatures seem
Ridiculous in the extreme.

The monk's behavior with his tail
Is something quite beyond the pale.

The camel chews a silly cud;
The hippo bathes in tropic mud.

The serpent never can resist
The tricks of the contortionist.

The whale, for all his glory, blows
Excessive water through his nose.

The idiotic fly will crawl
Along a ceiling or a wall.

But Man, who takes a higher track,
Is merely egomaniac.

   III. *The Sexes*

The sexes aren't very nice:
They are but instruments of vice.

If the obscure amoeba can
Get on without them, so should Man.

The dwellers in the pure serene
Are scrupulously epicene.

They play a little music, yes,
But merely out of blessedness.

Of course the Latin peoples are
Morally crepuscular.

But the Nordic will inherit
Heaven and earth for special merit.

A race so nobly destined ought
To propagate by power of thought—

Which the exalted Nordic can
More nearly do than any man.

For nothing is, as well you know,
But constant thinking makes it so.

IV. *Spiritual Revised*

Swoop low, sweet Spirit of St. Lou,
And lift me up into the blue.

Up through the cerulean floor
We'll float as through a cellar-door,

While envious rivals, hissing anger,
Glare upon our empty hangar.

God's natural gases will distil
Themselves our thirsty tanks to fill.

Into His pure domain we'll burst
Beatified, but also first.

The aviators of the Lord
Will lead us to our bright award.

And there, before the Throne, we'll make
A perfect landing for His sake.

And while the apocalyptic beast
Yields us his honors at the feast,

The *Times*, in an exclusive story,
Will print the record of our glory.

V. *The Parrot*

The parrot imitates the man
As nimbly as a parrot can.

He spreads his pinions green and red,
And trumpets for unleavened bread.

He doesn't worry, sweat or cuss
Because he's not mellifluous.

He doesn't care for music's laws—
A parrot simply caws be-cause.

A parrot caws the way he can,
Nor cares a caw for beast or man.

He lets his larynx take its course,
Although 'tis less a bird than hoarse.

Ah, I would give my absent pence
To have that bird's indifference!

'Tis I, Sir, Rhyming Rapidly

He who has not suffered away
The small perspective of the clay,
Or learned to hang his bleeding heart,
His trivial or heroic part,
His pain, his failure, or his might
Upon horizons infinite,
Shall chew the cud of every grief,
And all that will be, is, or was,
Shall dwindle to the bitter leaf,
The acrid herb, the nettled grass.

The marrow of his bones shall be
The savor of eternity,
And the gross fluid of his eye
Shall darken and confine his sky.
His year shall wither in a rose;
The mountain frustrate his desire,
And all the planetary woes
Circle his brain with lurid fire.
But he who dangles from his wrist
The rusty trinket of his life;
Whose mind is like a river-bed
Whereon the stream of peace and strife
Flows to the ocean of the dead,
Shall be the crowd, the Cross, the Christ.
His silent eye shall look afar

And see and also be the star.
Like earth, he shall possess the yield,
And be the walker and the field,
And pass his sorrows in the air,
And see his own joys flying there,
And beat, through every mortal part,
Harmonious with the central heart.

But who would be so richly poor,
And leave his brain's queer furniture
And the warm kitchen of his heart,
Naked and lone to go apart,
For the high mountain's wintry drouth,
And planets perching on his mouth,
And death juvescent in his veins,
And life, a sparrow in his bones,
Dropping his losses and his gains
Upon the pit's imagined stones?
Who would divorce the blood to lie
With pale peace illicitly,
Or only glacial silence hear
Instead of love and joy and fear
And hate and care and glassy dream,
To be the sparkle on a stream,
Or master of a nameless God,
Like flies and rocks and goldenrod,
Or the volcanic sundowns red,
Or the disentangled dead?
And who would see his skeleton
Dangle from moon and star and sun
In puppet rages, while he heard
The sheathèd sword, which is the Word,

Gnaw at its scabbard like a mouse,
And his own mind the empty house?

Drown in the howling autumn sea
Your serpent-cold philosophy,
And sing to the tormented blind
Desire in a corporeal wind,
And sing to the tormented sight
The convolutions of the light,
The tentacles of light, that seize
The unresisting void and mould
The vast bisexual hierarchies,
Whose aeons are sublunar gold,
Whose teeth and stomachs grow not old,
Who strum their platinum guitars,
And ride their comet motor-cars,
And tread both roses and the stars!
Sing of the blue, celestial buttes,
Which, desperate faith at first forecasting,
A special liturgy transmutes
Into Suburbia everlasting!
Sing of immortal life-extension,
Whose procreant tide engulfs the skies,
And add a mystic fourth dimension,
But merely as a compromise!
For what poor, mortal wretch would be
Healed of his hurt, except as he,
Or render the capacious dust,
With all his repetitious troubles,
Divine protraction of his lust
And heavenly blowing of his bubbles?
Pluck then, from your minor air

The worm that cancels every debt,
The root that strangles every care,
The wisdom that observes the fret
And fear and labor all around,
Like things that crawl upon the ground,
And blow upon your saxophone
A gusty and hilarious tone
Of golden ages, just ahead,
For Man evolved, and further on,
The loud and liquidated dead
Scrambling for vantage in the dawn:
The anteroom of heaven here
For the crowding, swindling rear;
The van upon the distant shore
Sweating, cheating evermore.

Well, Let's Include Them, Anyhow

I

You're a good boy; you mind your mother,
Your father, teacher, baby brother;
You put your pennies in the bankie,
And wipe your nosie on a hankie.
You don't go fighting, stealing, swearing—
You help your mother chop the herring.
Well, you grow up, and you continue
To show the kind of stuff that's in you:
You do not steal the boss's nickels;
You live on sour cream and pickles;
You take what comes and don't get sore yet,
Or ruin ruined women more yet—
And what thanks do you get for it? Can't you
    see yet?
Assassin, crook, you're asking *me* yet?

II

You go to bed; you can't sleep yet;
You decide to count a couple of sheep yet;
Well, you count ten; you count twenty;
You count more, you count plenty.
You find more sheep than you expected,
But there isn't one that you've neglected.
You waited while they stopped to browse yet;

166

You even counted stray cows yet;
You threw in lambs, you threw in rabbits;
You threw in goats with nervous habits.
Your head aches; your ears are humming—
And what thanks do you get? The sheep keep coming!

III

You've had your share of care and trouble,
Of debt and fret and sweat and stubble;
You've thought of death without a quiver
And tried to find a decent river.
You've drunk, let's say, the bitter cup yet,
But you've kept your chin and courage up yet;
You've carried on; the worst seems over;
You shout for joy, "Aha, clover!"
You see at last an honest measure
Of steaks and chops and sleep and pleasure—
And what do you get? Another clout yet—
You have to have your tonsils out yet!

IV

You have a girl, a real beauty,
A blend of housewife, pal and cutie;
A heaven, a hill, a star to fly to;
Your heart leaps, and *you* try to.
You go here, you go there yet—
With her you haven't a single care yet;
You dream this, you dream that yet,
You sit dreaming and get fat yet.
You call her "Tootsie," "Teeny-weeny,"
And feel at once like Mussolini.
No other man can make her budge yet;

167

She loves you too (or so you judge yet).
You know now why your life miscarried—
And what do you get? You get married!

V

You have a date to meet your sweetie;
You want to look so nice and neatie;
You want to cut a little dash yet,
And wish you had a waxed mustache yet.
Well, you start to shave and go on shaving
As if you had some inner craving;
You scrape away with classic valor
Till you get a positive prison pallor—
And what thanks do you get? Do you hear her
    rave yet?
She looks, and says you need a shave yet!

Ode, on the Construction of the Tallest Building in the World

~~~~~~

Lying awake and pondering the rent,
Hearing the jolly stars chant, "Six and eight
    per cent"
In all their up-to-date, melodious rings,
Through which a ticker sings,
Behold, I saw the Chrysler Building rise,
Most noble phallus that has yet essayed the skies,
And was content
With this, Man's last, supreme accomplishment.

Still pondering the rent, I sang for joy,
(Unmanly ways of the non-Nordic boy!)
To think that Chrysler had seduced the sky
And that we all should profit gloriously thereby;
That he had conquered with insistent stone
The shy, reluctant, virginal Unknown,
Who had rebuffed with antique chastity
Plato and Shakespeare, Beethoven and me,
And that we all should profit gloriously
    thereby!—
For who so mean he would not share
An empire vaster than sublunar air?
Nobody!—
And so I sang for joy,

(Being, as I said before, no Pilgrim Father's
     boy),
Chrysler would pay the rent
Out of the firmament—
The firmament that he had made his own
With one insistent thrust of virile stone—
Chrysler would surely pay the rent.
And I was quite content.

For now what need we further seek?
This is the world's peak;
This is the hilltop of the human climb;
This is the overtaking of swift Time;
This is the Grail, the glory of the quest;
The robe is rent, the Mystery possessed.
For has not Chrysler ravished the Unknown
With one deliberate thrust of phallic stone,
And made himself Jehovah's son-in-law?
Behold a common man has risen to this state,
The husband of the Sphinx and sovereign of
     Fate,
And sits beside Himself, as ringed with awe;
Has entered where poor Einstein could but peer!
Will he desert us now,
With seven concentric haloes on his brow,
The bridegroom of the once inviolable Bride?
Are we not with him risen
Out of this earthly prison;
Are we not sharers too of his divinity,
Who with a single thrust
Beatified his own and all our dust?
What is there more to suffer and to fear?

The Sphinx is riddled by a mortal man;
The frigid secret is possessed at last;
The door is closed on Man's concluded Past;
The hilly ages now are trodden down;
Chrysler has set the Apocalyptic crown
Upon the head of our tormented clan—
This Bridegroom of the once inviolable Bride,
So long aloof and now so gratified—
Never wore she with greater grace
The meditative night upon her face—
What if the Bank of Manhattan could but fail?
Hail, Chrysler, resolute, potent lover, hail!
Through you the torrent of our woe is spent.
Chrysler will pay the rent
Out of his portion of the firmament.
What even matters the rent?
Are we not now ascended from the sod
To be, through Chrysler, in-laws, yea, of God?
And so I lay content,
The struggle done,
The glory won.
The night waxed, then waned, like a high
    revelry.
The flaming Chryslers in the sky grew dim,
Which he had given to all the cherubim,
Who raced like children in them through the
    night,
To Chrysler's and his Bride's and Father-in-law's
    delight.
The dawn, new-washed for the festivity,
Moved like a bridesmaid in her hyacinthine
    white.

171

Followed the golden pages of the morn.
For once I rose and was not all forlorn.
Chrysler, I thought, will surely phone or write,
Or radio from the conquered skies
My personal share in this new paradise.
Chrysler will pay the rent.
In this new state of man there is no rent.
And so I was content.

Sounded the anvils of the metropolitan day.
Familiarly the hours roared away,
And in my diaphragm the old dismay
Began to sing God's mercies once again.
Has Chrysler thrust in vain?
Where is Chrysler, where is he,
That he has neither phoned nor radio'd me?
Has he ascended into Heaven alone?
And then I saw the mighty phallus rise
Firm against the somewhat drooping skies
And mirth succeeded moan.
This is no triumph one may make his own.
This is no individual ravishment.
This is the *world's* tallest building—no?
So!
This is the grand Apocalypse, foretold
In topaz, ruby, chalcedony, gold.
And so I am content,
And neither struggle, fret, nor pay the rent.
In fact, there is no rent.

I

Sometimes, since you must absent be,
I wish that Love would set me free;
I want to see you with my eyes;
I want to hold you with my hands,
But Thought itself too sorely tries
The heart with gossamer contrabands:—
You are far more than wandering air,
And nearer than the arrogant stars,
And no fair things are yet so fair
That they may be your avatars.
Come back, or let these others be;
Your shadows cannot comfort me:
You are the certain knife, not they,
To whittle my foolish life away!

II

Darling, you have lived and loved
And your capacious nature proved;
Now promise that the residue
To me will evermore be true!

Though you have been of much bereft,
Oh, give me, give me what is left,
And let me ever, ever be
The keeper of the moiety!

173

Oh, promise, promise to be true!—
I love the fraction that is you;
And let, past all subtraction, me
Your final numerator be!

III

The interfering stars above
Decree that we must part,
So, fare you well, my loveliest love,
With, I suppose, my heart.

And I shall grieve for you, my sweet—
For who is truly wise?—
Though all the sour facts repeat
That blessings love disguise.

Oh, other joys, they say, abound
In thoughtful Man's estate,
But Love still makes the world go round
That else were going straight.

IV

Stand not too near me,
Lest in time arise
A need of the nearness
Of your hands and eyes;

Of the words of your mouth,
Of your care, your caress,
Of the staff and the scrip
Of your tenderness.

When the great, central cloud
That domes the doomed world
Is rent like a tent-cloth,
And the storm-spears are hurled—

The lightnings of sorrow,
The wild arrows of pain—
Let me not need your nearness,
Lest I need in vain.

Let me stand lonely
By the dark, still deep,
Lest I call you, only,
Only to weep.

My own is my pain,
My own is my fear;
Frail are we to sustain:
Stand not too near.

V

If the truth were not so hard,
You might say this thing to me,
That you made me shard by shard
Out of ruins tremblingly—

Out of fragments that remained
In your heart of other days;
Out of knowledge that you gained
When you walked on sweeter ways.

175

I am what the rest were not;
I am not myself at all;
I am something you have wrought
Like a vase upon the wall.

Well, I'll ever be on guard,
And I'll safely play the game,
Lest I crumble shard by shard
And you cry some dearer name.

VI

Ah, the house that we shall build
In our love's fair weather!
Ah, the many fields untilled
We shall till together!

We shall build and till and reap,
Singing in all weather;
Then, at last, we'll go to sleep,
Possibly, together.

VII

Your hair is so golden;
Your hair is my joy,
Like Helen's in olden
High splendor of Troy.

I wonder how true are
Such portents; I—well,
I wonder if you are
As fickle as Hel—!

VIII

How long, how long, are the days without you!
How lone the light, how far the faces!
You have gathered the quickness of earth about
    you
And left a death upon people and places.

As in a dream I walk, I wander,
Seeing your face in all the faces,
Until in my arms we kiss and ponder
A happy choice of people and places.

IX

I love my love
That she is woman;
I fear my love
That she is human.

Ah, were she woman
One shade less,
She would not so
My heart oppress;

But were she free
Of any fault,
She would not so
My heart exalt.

X

You love me and I love you,
Yet one and one make always two.

How bright the light from every sun,
If one and one made ever one!

XI

Please remember that you are,
Though we never meet again,
Compounded of a song and star
And a madness in my brain.

XII

Oh, had you but tarried!
Oh, had you but waited!
Oh, had we not married!—
Although it was fated!—

What dreams in our bosom
Now might we not carry
Of sunshine and blosson
When we two should marry!

XIII

Loving me, be not too faint
To observe and bear in mind
Every reason for complaint:
Be not to my faults too blind;

So that, when you prepare to go,
You can say with righteous pride:
"You did so-and-so-and-so,"
And be sweetly justified.

XIV

Love, a little of myself
I'll keep: you have enough of pelf;
You will not grudge my heart the pence
It saves against your going hence.

When next autumn's leaves are shed,
My soul shall need both meat and bread;
You will have much richer loot,
And I shall not go destitute.

Metaphysical

The Lord is in the sea and sky;
The Lord is in the rose and root;
The Lord is in my shirt and tie,
My dentist and my either boot;
The Lord is in the earth and air—
In short the Lord is everywhere.

For if He were not everywhere,
He could not then look out for us,
And if He were not everywhere,
He would not be ubiquitous,
And that—but then you know as well
As I, that is unthinka-bel.

And since He is ubiquitous,
The Lord is in my creditors;
And since He is ubiquitous,
The Lord is in those editors
Who tell me it is blasphemous
To sing Him so ubiquitous.

He is the germ ubiquitous,
The cures and the preventatives,
The preacher and the 'potamus,
The House of Representatives,

And that—but then you know as well
As I—that is unthinka-bel.

If He were not ubiquitous,
He could not then look out for us,
But if He is, He'd have to be
In you, of course, and even me,
And that is so preposterous
It verges on the blasphemous.

Consider the dilemma He
Provides for His apologist!
For which the only remedy
Is here appended, I insist:
There's so much wrong with everything,
The Lord has quit ubiquit-ing!

I

The ocean spills upon the sands
Water with a thousand hands,
And when the water all is spilled,
The sands are dry, the ocean filled.

II. *Aubade: New York*

Now Morning, blue and golden, falls
On Bloch and Finkel Overalls;
Incarnadines with bold advance
The front of Blaustein's Kiddie Pants,
And stoops to sample with a kiss
The truth of Cleanso Dentifrice.
Then, tripping smartly on her way
In crêpe that rustles Paul Poiret,
Her lovely mouth all redolent
Of Listerine and Pepsodent,
Her hair in wavelets that evince
The art of Louis, Cat and Quince,
At last her Onyx footfalls come
To Lucky Strike and Wrigley's gum,
Where pausing, half prepared to swoon,
She wishes it were never noon.

Sweet Morning, ere you yield the boon
Of heaven to the afternoon,
Oh, let me envy from the ground
The sights of your celestial round!
How pleasant from your height of East
Your eyes on such delight to feast;
To learn that Lifebuoy floats and laves;
That Kelly Tires while Pluto saves;
That tubes of Forhan's hourly strive
To add four more and make it five;
That beards are never what they seem
To hopeful Colgate's Shaving Cream;
That men will gladly suffer much
And more, for Skins They Love to Touch;
That Zoolac is no vulgar milk;
That Moon-Glo has become a silk;
That Gloria Swanson, shining far,
Is still your sister, and a star!

Sweet Morning, wandering in Thibet,
Can you forget, can you forget?
Do you, unmindful, never stop
To weep regret for Autostrop,
Or seek among some crag of Alp
Ed. Pinaud in a tourist-scalp?
Or when your orient sandals brave
The Cashmere wild, the Caspian wave,
Do you not yearn to lay your heart
On Roxy's Synagogue of Art?
Where, by the lone and febrile Nile,
Do jolly natives walk a mile
Through sands more dread than northern mud

To see the Camel chew his cud,
Or where dare palm and olive hope
To mate and conquer while there's soap?

Dear Morning, in our western night,
I see your golden car alight
On a pagoda-roof, below
The cherry's fragrant spring of snow,
Because Uneeda Biscuit so,
And thus refreshed, dream longingly
Of that tall city by the sea
Where sons of Halitosis fight
The spectral battle day and night,
And having struggled, having won,
Climb to their places in the sun.

III

Like lidless eyes, the windows stare
On people, street and empty air;
On happiness and misery,
They seem to gaze impartially;
And yet, I cannot help but think
That sometimes they would like to wink,
Or shut their lids at all they see
Of folly and of vanity.
To stare at all the suns and rains
And men, should give them window-panes.

IV

The backs of houses in the rain
Are sad as dreams one dreams in vain;
Are sad as memories that waken

184

Thoughts of the lovely road not taken.
So drooping-still, so lone are they,
So melancholy and so gray,
It seems such selfishness and sin
Not to take the poor things in,
And let them look, at any rate,
On the small solace of a grate.
But then, the downcast are such bores,
They don't deserve a place indoors.
Who are as futile as a mouse is,
Deserve to be just backs of houses.

V

Lamplight, through a leafy lace
Of trees, has a surprising grace:
The family in evening ease
I picture through the tinted trees;
The father with his sheaf of papers,
The children with their pretty capers,
And mother, fresh and sane as wheat,
Sewing with fingers love makes fleet.
How such a scene would taunt the devil,
If it were only on the level!

VI

Cross-legged where the lamplight gleams
A bronze and silent Buddha dreams,
With placid and metallic pity
For all the turmoil of the city,
As if, although his eyes are blind,
He saw the stress of humankind.
I gaze at him and wish that he

Would lend me his serenity—
That imperturbable repose
'Round which the sea of Gotham flows
And breaks like water on a rock;
The bronze victorious in the shock.
But sometimes, when in merry fettle,
I'd rather suffer than be metal.

VII. *Sheep*

Nibble, nibble, little sheep,
In the meadow, on the steep;
Keep your nozzle in the grass
And let the Kingdom come to pass.

All the money in the mint,
All the news that's fit to print
Is but grass upon the steep
For another kind of sheep.

You have ticks and fleas, I know;
They have *sum* and *cogito*;
You are prey to simple bites;
They have transatlantic flights.

Happy, happy, little sheep,
You have but to eat and sleep;
Even when you ruminate
Saint Peter dozes by the gate.

They have radio, submarines,
Complexes and endocrines,

Television, taxes, rent,
Faith and hope and six per cent.

You are casual with your kind;
They have organized a mind;
You are mated for a goal;
They have libido and soul.

You are sexed for simple use;
They have let their women loose;
Earth remembers you and yields
Milk of her mammalian fields.

There is but a line between
You and your nutritious green,
But to get their grass they must
Scrabble riddles in the dust;

Scrabble riddles on their brain,
Make a plow of wind and rain,
Bury stars and pile up stone,
Bind their hearts and yoke their own.

When the shearer's work is done
Yours the pasture and the sun;
But for them the unborn years
Are but whetstones for the shears.

You see what your eyes command—
Cloud and clover, lake and land,
But their sight must lag behind
The laboring oxen of the mind.

Nibble, nibble, little sheep,
In the meadow, on the steep;
When the Kingdom comes to pass,
Its tents and trumpets will be grass.

VIII. *Cloud*

The cloud assumes fantastic shapes
Of beasts and continents and capes;
Of island, mountain, monolith,
And hybrid fauna out of myth.
I've seen the knights of Arthur's court
Themselves among its towers disport;
The silver griffon charge the sun,
And once, a gold Napoleon.

Alas, that hot ambition leaps
The steed that walks, the man who creeps,
And girt for conquest of the sky,
Conspires with creatures born to die!
The turret thins; the dream is done;
A breeze dissolves Napoleon;
The griffon curls his pale remains
Round Arthur's court, while Arthur rains.

Myself have charged the hilly morn
A metaphoric unicorn;
Have hung upon my airy heart
A hybrid bard and Bonaparte;
Have stormed in fabled length and flight
The lunar headlands of delight,

And laid fantastic paws along
The foam-edge of the isles of song.

And yet there died upon the sky
A sun-struck vapor that was I,
And left no mark of myth or man
Or bard or quasi-Corsican.
Desirous cloud, we are too wan
For day or night to build upon,
And all our dream of happiness
Goes up in steam, comes down in less!

IX. *Hill*

From the grassy path we turn
Through thorny vine and crowded fern,
Through sumach waiting for the brand,
And the green tangle of the land,
Because the hill persuades the eye
With promise of a wider sky.

And then we gain the shallow crest
And take our disappointed rest,
And see with all our aching mind
The brambled wild we left behind,
And search with all the wandering eye
A heaven no bluer, and as high.

Ever before, the earth-strong briar,
The sumach thirsting for the fire,
The unconquered place we struggled through;

189

Ever behind, a gypsy blue
That leans upon a hill and lies
To the quick heart and gallant eyes.

Ever and evermore, until
The grave arises like a hill
Around us and surmounts desire,
The opposing and sardonic briar,
The hill beyond, the lying crest,
The impassive heaven, the restless rest.

X

A little while to love and rave
And fret and sweat and fear and hope in;
A little while to bathe and shave
And keep the organism open—
Then silence under reeds and roses,
And no more blowing of our noses.

A little while to sweat and bleed
For cheese and biscuits on a table;
A little while to spill our seed
As per directions on the label—
Then dust and wind for saint and sinner,
And no bicarb to praise our dinner.

A little while to give a maid
The things she wants to make her sadder;
A little while to make the grade
Bestrewn with gravel from the bladder—
Then weeds and grass that cows will edit,
And no more cash, and no more credit.

190

A little while to sleep, or lie
Suspended by some weird psychosis;
To strut, or search the wandering eye
For proof of dreaded halitosis—
Then let the process-servers find us,
Our dental bridges far behind us!

Oh, Lord, who had the right idea
To tame our pride and sex and stomachs;
Who matched our teeth with pyorrhea,
Our tallest towers with graveyard hummocks—
Accept my praises now—I'd rather
Never meet the gifted Author!

XI

I've been in love a dozen times,
And fashioned several thousand rhymes;
For love I've suffered much, indeed,
And rhyming makes my spirit bleed;
And yet, I have unhappy times
When I am out of love and rhymes.

XII

When I had your love, my heart
Was lifted spears and burning banners;
I swaggered through the streets of art
And song, with all a conqueror's manners.

I was the confidant of Fate,
(Who plays such nubile tricks upon us),
I had no envy of the great,
Or malice even for Adonis.

But when I lost your love, I found
My conquest was but breath and bubble;
I walked upon prosaic ground
Whose yield, it seemed, was chiefly stubble.

And then I grieved in purse and pride
That when I was so high and mighty,
I didn't set some store aside
Against the day when you'd be flighty.

XIII

There is no place where I would stray;
There is no place where I would stay;
My soul is dark with stormy riot,
Directly traceable to diet.
I'm sorry that the spirit's treasons
Should spring from such material reasons!

XIV

Sometimes, I think I'd like to be
A student of zoology,
To know the day-dreams of the auk,
And why the balky mule must balk;
To learn what the rhinoceros
And emu have to say to us.
I think I'd like to understand
Why camels love to play in sand,
And why the zebra has to look
Like a picture in a book.
But most of all, I'd like to know
How the human race got so.

XV

I'm sorry for the people pent
In grimy cities, slaves of Rent,
Who need a thousand eyes and feet
To get across a simple street;
Who never see the so-called sky,
And are too tired to live or die.
They're far less fortunate than cows
That peacefully in pastures browse,
And tranquilly the milk-pail fill,
Earning their living standing still.
I wish these people all could go
Where the untrammelled breezes blow,
And lambs and calves and other pups
Nibble at the buttercups.
I wish they all could go away
And watch the stripling fishes play
Where other gods are served than Pelf:
I need the extra room myself.

XVI

Calmly, in the commissary mead
The cows, the calves, the sheep, the lambkins feed;
They nibble as their noses list what chow
The field provides for sheep and lamb and cow;
They turn no sniffing bugles up to say,
"Waiter, what's on the bill-of-fare today?"
Or weigh with worry and unspoken curse
The monstrous price against the puny purse.
The laden landscape offers its cuisine:
They view the prospect and consume the scene.

No hoof to mouth their happy state disturbs;
No minatory tip their pleasure curbs;
What's underfoot is quickly under way,
Without a cover charge, (or cabaret),
Which we, who come to scoff, remain to pay.
Oh, creatures noble in your simple lot,
And even nobler when you go to pot,
These acres of green grass are yours to eat;
Go to it, creatures—it improves the meat!

XVII

When I was young, (or maybe, five),
And glad, so glad to be alive,
Oh, how my fancy used to itch
To be—how shall I put it?—rich!
A millionaire, it seemed to me,
Was quite the only thing to be;
A millionaire or billionaire
Or trillionaire—let's leave it there!
Well, now my jolly youth is dead,
My pretty, infant fancies fled,
And here I sit and brood and itch
To be—how shall I put it?—rich!

XVIII

When all alone at night I lie
And stare upon a square of sky,
A wanderer by the wind-worn deep
Where all must walk who cannot sleep,
Who goes with me along the strand
And holds my limp and fevered hand?

194

Who stays with me the slow night through,
My lone and loyal retinue,
And guards me till the break of day?
My friend, my pal, Insom-ni-ay!

XIX

When winter's here, my thoughts revert
To the phenomena of dirt;
In short, in fact, or what you will,
I think of meadow, grove and hill;
Of the inevitable rose,
And almost anything that grows:
(I cannot catalogue them all,
Because my store of facts is small).
I also wander, wide and free,
The realm of ornithology,
And fill my dreaming mind with herds,
Or swarms, or droves, or flocks of birds.
In brief, when winter's here, I grow
Bucolic as a garden hoe.
But when the spring begins to lay
Her carpet on the meanest way,
And buds bestar the humid air
Not only here, but everywhere,
And robins leap, and pastures glow,
And so and so and so and so,
My love of Nature, here set down,
Deserts me, and I stick in town;
Which demonstrates that oftentime
(At least for purposes of rhyme),
A wandering bird in No Man's Land
Is worth a spring-full in the hand.

XX

Who stares upon a star too long,
Will see a woman and hear a song,
And when the night of gazing's done,
He'll think he sees her under the sun,
Because his star-struck mind will be
Dazed with the dead night's ecstasy.
The woman will break his heart in two;
The song will eat his brain right through.

XXI

Lovely you seem, and yet I know
My feeble thinking makes it so;
My foolish heart that shuns despair,
Flies to your breast and calls you fair.
I see you clearly as you are,
And have to call you sun and star,
Because I am so dead afraid
Of an even deeper shade.
You know all this, and smile, and love it,
And take absurd advantage of it.
Alas, that the more tender human
Has nothing else to love but woman!

XXII. *On the Death of a Distinguished Statesman*

He's gone, and all the world weeps by his bier,
According to the press—
(Though I have failed to find a single tear,
Or symptom of distress:—
Therefore, I take this meaning in the rough—
The bier is metaphoric, home-brew stuff).

196

Well, anyhow, he's dead, the mighty man,
And here we are
A metaphorically mourning clan
Lamenting his extinguished star,
Bowed in the glory of his lasting name.
(Yet Monday follows Sunday just the same!)
Alas, we all must go,
In human destiny:—
Cæsar is dead, and oh,
What difference to me?

Complex, with Victim Victorious

I have no homeland;
I have no Saviour;
I live among people
Of different behaviour;
I have no army,
I have no navy
To rattle their victories,
Stand by, and save me.

When I make blunders
Of act or omission,
I have no aegis
Of custom, tradition—
Chiefs or apostles
To ward off the dangers:
When I am strange,
I am strange among strangers.

Oh, to be different
Breeds heartache and trouble!
But he who is strange
Among strangers pays double.
I have no banner
To fly from my passion,
No gentry to set
My caprices in fashion.

For a half-note of music
I stole from the spheres,
I must weep double
The alien's tears;
I must be two times
The stranger, it seems—
Once for my people,
And once for my dreams.

For a petal of beauty
I shook from the tree
Whose leaves are the moonlight,
Whose roots are the sea,
I stand in the thunder-still
Darkness and strip
For death without burial
And love with a whip.

The lover who follows
The feet of the spheres,
Shall wrestle with shadows
And die on their spears;
But woe to him doubly,
And double his loss,
If he have nor an army,
A navy, a Cross!

An army and navy
To fight for the Lord,
And acres and customs
Enriched by the sword—

His music will dwindle,
His petal will die,
And he may not take it
As lightly as I.

The Moist Land

(Being an account of the flight of Mr. T. S. Eliot from Scotland into Shropshire, from Shropshire into Wales, and thence into the Irish Sea.)

Unum, duo, tres, quattuor, quinque, sex, septem, octo, novem, decem; shema yisrael, adonai alohainu adonai echad; nun Wilhelm, wie geht's in der Schule, ganz gut, papa; ibid, infra dig, anon, sic, anno mirabile.

I. The Demobilization of the Fleet

April's very fickle following
March which is very windy, following
February, very sleety, following
December, and so next year is this year
And so forth and so forth and so forth,
Etcetera, und so weiter.
The Archduke in scarlet hunting coat came down to
    breakfast
Having slept all night with his hunting-boots under
    the sheets
His gun by his side. The steel of the barrel glittered
All night like phosphorescence in the room heavy with
    panatelas.
"Officer, which way is uptown, and if so which way is
    downtown?

I am a widow woman from Lynn, Massachusetts, and
    have never been here before,
Though I have a cousin on the force whose name is
    Sweeney,
A Titanic fellow, big I mean, bronzed as iodine,
Do you know him perhaps?
Perhaps, perchance, haply, mayhap, maybe?
Yes, no, nein, ja, oui, si, non?"
"My own name is Schultz. No Sweeney do I know."
"And yet my own husband was German. I am as I
    said a widow woman."

In Hamburg an der Elbe
Da schwimmt ein Krokodil.

Now gleam the birches ghost-white wherever they are.
The sacerdotal poplars seem to have taken off their
    surplices
Against the heat. What time is it, Nathan?
Quelle heure est-il? Or, is the Big Ben out of order
    again?
The perch season is open in eastern West Virginia,
Give me a silver arrow and a bow of polished tin,
Give me a cross-bow out of Thessaly or Irkutsk,
Or an old-fashioned Winchester such as pawnbrokers
    still use in Erie, Pa., against burglars,
And I will prick their shins in the delicate mine-water,
The dirty perch!
How long, oh, Catiline, will you keep up this pish-posh?

Come, Marie, let us go to the Moscow Art Theatre.
Zhil ya na Tiflise

Bil ya na Kavkase.
Closer, Marie (is not that Mischa Elman going into
    the shop to buy rosin—
He is a short fellow for his height, don't you think?)
Come closer, and we shall watch the moon rise over
    Tammany Hall.
The violins begin, let us imagine they are nightingales,
Singing their last, for the world ends tomorrow.
(About this time the fat-legged chorus comes on; do
    they still say, "So this is Paris"?)
Come, we will stand on the corner of Fourteenth
    Street and Third Avenue.
The world is falling about us like a whole autumn;
Come close, in the shadow, in the shadow,
The shadow that lengthens and lengthens,
As if we stood under the legs of a Colossus.
My heart is broken, Marie; the moon is red
With blood. And I wonder, I wonder,
Which six of the seven cities that claimed Homer
    were liars?
Comment allez-vous? Très bien, Monsieur.

II. A *Three-Handed Game of Pinochle*

Antiques, Madame? The Modern Antique Company
Has been in business forty-seven years
And never one dissatisfied customer.
Benvenuto! Benvenuto Cellini!
Tarry a moment, it is I, Fra Lippo Lippi,
There are two damsels in the cemetery
Waiting for us under the cypresses;
Let's go together.

Chi troppo sale
Precipitevolissimevolmente.
Flow softly, Wabash, till I end my song!
"Oh, God, how I hate things out of Grand Rapids!"
Have you ever known what it is to hunger for objects
    d'art?
This candelabra, *par exemple,* pray
Examine it; observe this little stain—
This little copper stain—well, it was blood.
"Do you remember the Marchesa—
The little fiery woman out of Bologna?
No? Well, we'll say no more about it!"
"Have you ever been lost in the Schwarzwald,
    Amalie,
With nothing to eat but those filthy little sausages
They sell in Köln at Schimmel's there on the corner?"

"What was that?"

        "I shouldn't be surprised
If dead men tell no tales."
"I think we've been dead a hundred thousand years."

"Yes, and I know that was Little Red Riding Hood
I saw today on Fort Washington Avenue."
Aloha! Aloha!
But the barges spread sail down the river like
    peacocks,
Their canopies of orange and azure,
A sailor from Smyrna with a lemon between his
    teeth

Fell into the water. O there, Demetrios!
"I think you got a nerve, Mr. Rosenzweig, to ask I
    should marry your daughter without a dowry."
In Hongkong I met Kwong Chu,
A mandarin with fingernails a yard long.
He had the most exquisite manners,
And I shall never forget his beautiful angel's smile
When he had us to tea that afternoon in January,
An hour after he had decapitated his mother.
Flow gently, Wabash, till I end my song.
IT'S A QUARTER TO FOUR!
"Is you comin', Andrew Jackson?"
"I ain't sayin' as I ain't."

"I ain't askin' yuh as you ain't; I'se askin' you as
    yuh is.
Now is yuh?"
IT'S A QUARTER TO FOUR.

Have you met Nastasia Fillipovna, I said,
And he said he hadn't, so I asked him to.
And that was the beginning. She was one
Of those fierce Russian women, knows no fun.
Hurry up, Johnny, and get your gun.
Well, in a week the man was done for.
IT'S A QUARTER TO FOUR.
For God's sake, will somebody sing Dardanella!
IT'S A QUARTER TO FOUR.
Good-night, ladies,
Good-night, ladies,
Good-night, ladies,
We're going to leave you now.

205

By the way, I'm sure you know the Côte d'*azur*.
IT'S A QUARTER TO FOUR.
As for me, I never took anything stronger
Than a thimbleful of rum
Even in the good old days,
But you, Mr. O'Brien, say you drink hair-tonic.
Flow softly, Wabash, till I end my song.

III. *Death by Hooch*

I am the same, Panthides,
I, Leotychides, who once in Elymais
Herded black sheep and by Hypanis shore,
Looking on Thebes a thousand leagues away,
Wreathed for your head a crown of eglantine,
And drank a copper keg of home-made wine.

Hula, hula,
Hula, hula,
Old Mother Hubbard she made my bed.
But what good is it
Since Ivan the Terrible
The Brooklyn Bridge
And Staten Island
Fell on my head?

Oh, Carthage, Carthage,
What boots it that the hawthorns keep their snows
Against these many months of wind and sun?
I resolved to take only sarsaparilla,
But what good did that do?

The clerk dished me up a vanilla,
Believing Columbus a Jew.

Take these, *les fleurs mourantes, mademoiselle.*
There's nothing more for me to say,
(Oh, Neptune, Neptune, call your mermaids in!)
Until you get my letter.
But I know
(*Oi, weh is mir, weh is mir!*)
That they've christened
Petrograd
Something or other,
And there's nothing to do
Until somebody
Can find my brother.
The more's the pity,
He's gone, he's gone
In a Spanish galleon
With Henry VIII
To Atlantic City.

La, la,
I've waited in High Bridge,
But I'm going now.

Rome is burning,
Yes, burning,
Gott
im
Himmel,
burning,

burning,
hula, hula,
la, la.

IV. *Thunder and Lightning*

The dead are living
And the living are dead
And there's no use in giving
Your board and your bed
To the sorrowful woman who came
From Lithuania
Latvia
Vienna or Rumania
Rome or Czecho-Slovakia
With an instep and eyebrows of flame.
Waiki, waiki.
What if I have three keys to my apartment
One gold, one silver and one lead
Here in this desert place the frogs are withered
The griffons are no bigger than fleas,
The sands are rocky and the rocks are sandy,
And there's not enough water
And not enough brandy
To wash the ears of King Cole's daughter.
Co co lo co po co.
   Oh if there were
Oh if there were
   Oh if there were
Do do do do do do
Ra mi fa so.

Let her sit at her piano and play Tschaikowsky,
But we who know how black the sun can be
Yom Kipper Eve or when there is no sun at all
We'll wait in this dead land and see
The Woolworth Building fall.

They will be here presently
And we shall be parched and shrivelled,
Whoever they are we shall be blanched and withered.
We have only to say coo coo
And all will be over.
Even the unicorns stay in their dry holes
The vampires mourn. Wait till the thunder speaks
Dada, goo goo
Abracadabra.
My friend you see me dead and yet I know
I have not long to live
After the purple gnats with bovine faces
After Jerusalem's fallen and Mrs. Grundy
Comes by on a black horse with the three graces.
Gautama's gone, the sacred bull is gone.
Apis is gone
Adio, bella Napoli, adio
Adio
Wait Khiva till the Ganges turns to milk,
You'll hear the tiger laugh with green grimaces
You'll see the thunder lift the Himalayas
As if they were a toothpick.
Da da ma ma pa pa
HALLELUJAH
I'll wait awhile for Julian the Apostate

209

You go and pick the fallen lightnings up
And see if Mrs. Porter
Has got enough soda water.

Farewell, I've turned the prow to Greece again.
Shall I call up my lawyer, Cortlandt 0004
And say the sea is beautiful tonight.
Brooklyn Bridge is falling down falling down falling
    down

Amo amas amat amabo amabimus
Huius huius huius—O mea culpa
There's never anything to say though I should say
The less the more. The blue parrot's fainted.
God bless you all. Paracelsus is drunk again.
Daddy, Damdaddy. Damdaddy

Shanty shanty shanty.

Rag-Bag

I. *Landscape*

Since there is little rain, and since
The days hang dry as leaves in drouth,
I have no words to write that mince,
Or burn like summers in the South.

A hard road and frozen puddles,
A slate evening overlong,
And now and then a bird that muddles
Something born to be a song.

Stubblefields on either hand,
A house, a human figure moving
In all the greyness of the land
Through dull labor and tasteless loving.

This is the landscape of this life;
This is the core you've bitten to;
This is the fruit of fear and strife;
This is the seed from which it grew.

And when you've eaten the apple's meat,
And spat the seed upon the ground,
You'll squat through a little cold and heat
While Silence slowly strangles Sound.

II. *Observation*

Little by little we subtract
Faith and Fallacy from Fact,
The Illusory from the True,
And starve upon the Residue.

What is the sense in tears or laughter?
The Root of things is what we're after:
But fallen trees will spill their fruit
And worms and darkness keep the root.

Fallen days will spill their sun,
But paper heavens must be won,
And so, while we geometrize,
A bird out-twits us, twice as wise.

Mere matter is not all of marrow;
The harvest leaps not from the harrow,
And a push-button will not light
Joy by day, or stars by night.

III. *The Last Religion*

Since now the several churches
Have left their sour communicants in
      various lurches,
And since Jehovah does not turn a hair
At individual or amalgamated prayer;
Since, nevertheless, the heart demands
More than the fruit of earth, machines or
      hands,

Than bread or bed alone,
Let us construct an idol of our own—
Something to cling to when the dead leaves
    fall,
To warm the windy air above the sea,
To dull the edges of futility
And sit with in the shadow of the pall.

In the dark field of our despair,
In the long, perplexed, tormented night,
Where there is neither road nor light,
We may hear it moving there,
Dull hoofs on dry grass,
Among the living and bewildered dead;
Then hear it braying like an ass
And be suddenly comforted.

IV. *The Shelves of the World*

The shelves of the world
Have much to show—
The way of the worm,
The why of snow;

Kings and rivers,
Queens and trees,
Men and gods
And beasts and bees;

Cloven hills,
Uncovered woods,

Plato's thoughts
And Buddha's moods.

And when I've read
Until I'm blind,
And jewels glisten
In my mind,

Their covenant still
The stars will keep
Of silence with
The sullen deep.

And when I've read
For threescore years,
The speech of Sorrow
Will still be tears.

V. *Wind, Rain, Fire*

Wind, blow the rain about;
Twist and tear the threaded drops;
Night, be dark as disillusioned days!

Within, I spin my thought beside
The salty sea-wood burning green
And creamy, fragrant apple-branches red.

Lash, wind; tumble, rain!
So do the blind and maniac gods
Strike at the puny, human foe below,

Who, for safety and defence,
Builds his fires and spins his thought
By sea-wood burning green and apple red.

Burn, fires, red and green;
Spin, thought, your life and death;
Lash, wind; tumble, rain; strike, gods!

And you, with tempest-bandaged eyes,
Wandering stars and seraphim,
Swim clear, without fear, the brawling sea!

Human eyes and human hands
Beside the burning green and red
See for you and guide you through the night.

VI. *Allegory*

When one has broken, say thirty acres,
And thirty acres have broken one, too,
And the plow stands cliff-like before the
    striving,
And endless labor is yet to do:

Acres and acres still to harrow,
Rocks to cut from their flesh of sod,
The very worm that crawls in the furrow,
The broken spirit will call it God;

The worm that crawls in the chain-like
    furrow,
The night that falls on the hostile sod,

The stars, the stillness, a lamp and linen,
The tired spirit willl call it God.

Whatever comes not to bruise and break
      him;
Whatever stands not with naked sword:
A worm, a leaf, a light, a window,
The routed spirit will call it Lord.

He will curse the seed, he will hate the
      furrow,
And all that springs from the stony sod;
But the twig in the road that gives or takes
      not,
The frightened spirit will call it God.

When one has struggled with thirty acres—
A year an acre of bitter clod,
The dark that folds him, the dust that
      covers,
The broken spirit will call it God.

   VII. *The Word*

Only one thing knows
The Word that I seek—
A thing wide as the earth is,
Yet a small thing and meek.

It knows more than the stars together,
And a lifetime of flowers,

And the priests drunk by their altars,
And the grey and golden hours.

And many I know have found it,
Found it, and heard
In a great, victorious moment
The Apocalyptic Word;

Have heard the little cat-mouth
Of the yawning grave speak,
And followed the Word forever—
The Word that I seek.

VIII. *Consolation*

I had a sorrow
That ate away
The heart of night
And the brain of day.

Ah, here was a sorrow
To rid me of!
And I said, "Remember,
The earth is love;

"The world is acid
And hate and steel,
But the earth will reach
Her hand and heal."

So I sat with the hills
Till the sun went down

217

And the stars came fleeing
From the town.

And when the dark
Was still as stone,
The grief of the hills
Was like my own.

So I took my sorrow
Into a wood
And heard the word
Of the solitude,

And stared at a bush,
And stared at a tree,
Till the eyes walked out
Of the body of me.

And when I saw
Nor bush nor tree,
The sorrow remained
Inside of me.

IX. *Proposal*

I bring you truce for your desire;
I bring you negativities,
And on a globe, to cool your fire,
The shrivelled continents and hollow seas.

The golden bowl, the silver cord
I bring you as a minatory sign,

And for your strength, a broken sword,
And for your sea-dream, taste of brine.

Would you have more—the bubbles blown
Under the cloud? The rainbow's end?
Let me go on alone, alone:
I asked to be your friend!

X. *Hymn*

He comes at last into the shade
Where men and women weep;
He gives the lover to his maid,
The shepherd to his sheep.

His presence calms the weeping wild
Of the confusèd throng;
He gives the mother to her child,
The poet to his song.

Peace to the broken heart He brings,
And to the mind repose;
He gives the bird untiring wings,
And summer to the rose.

And though His staff is like a sword,
And like a cloud His breath,
How shall we hail His coming, Lord,
That guise of You called Death?

XI. *The Garment*

I shall stand before God
In no man's coat,
Nor pluck the praise
From another's throat.

The priests may lock
Their sacristies,
For none of their garments
My taste shall please.

Though broken and halting
Be my strain,
The psalmists shall offer
Their songs in vain.

The robe I shall wear
Myself have wrought
Of the reeds of my life
And the rose of my thought.

Though the monk go gowned
In a richer cloth,
The good Lord's pity
Forgive us both.

XII. *Kin*

Out of what air flows sorrow?
Out of what fountain tears?

Not of the night or morrow;
Not of the streaming years.

The night is bright and starry;
The heavens utter sleep;
Whence are the winds that carry
Tears for my eyes to weep?

The morning launches merry
Her ship of rose and gold;
Whence are the spirits that carry
Stones for my heart to hold?

They are my sister and brother;
They are my kith and kind;
Out of the womb of my mother
They leaped into my mind.

XIII. *Symbol*

When you come back to me, belovèd;
When you come back to me,
I, who may walk the wide world over,
Shall only then be free.

When you have bound me fast in fetters,
The fetters of your love,
I shall be free as waves in water,
And birds in air above.

I shall be free as growing trees are,
Whose roots are deep in ground;

That yet have all the air for kingdom,
By Heaven's love unbound.

I shall be free as hills whose bases
In earthy dungeons rest,
Whom Heaven lifts up with lovingkindness
To lean upon her breast.

I, who may walk the wide world over,
Who now am seeming free,
May never leave my heart's deep prison
Until you turn the key:

Until your voice, like Joshua's trumpets,
Sounding my great release,
Blow down my loneliness, my longing,
And I walk forth to peace.

I. *Spiritual*

I got a complex; you got a complex—
All God's chillun got things.
You are neurotic; I got suppressions;
She's idiotic; *they* owe money—
All God's chillun got things.

Heb'n! Heb'n!
M'yeh, Heb'n!

I got a summons; you got sinus trouble—
All God's chillun got things.
You are a book-keeper; I am worse off;
She *can't* get married; he *got* married—
All God's chillun got things.

Heb'n! Heb'n!
Go tell papa!

II. *Mother and Child*

(A penetrating study of the psychology of the Younger Generation and its Parents, in the carefully-transcribed idiom of contemporary New York. This may prove a very valuable document. Please hold it.)

Mommer, oo, how bloo I feel!
Wassamatter, baby?
I ain't got no sex appeal,
And never won't have, maybe.

Baby, waddayeh mean yeh ain't?
Now you are on'y six yet;
Wot yeh got is summer complaint,
Wich the doctor will come 'n fix yet.

Mommer, dear, I ain't no heel,
An' you're talkin' like a moron;
I ain't got no sex appeal
An' I wish I never was boron!

Baby, you're a pain in the neck!
An' Mommer, you're another!
Baby, you are full of sec-
S appeal, just like your mother.

Elinor Glyn should meet yeh yet,
An' maybe yeh wouldn't stop 'er!
An' I wish I could say as much, yeh bet,
About yer dear old popper.

If 'e on'y had a little bit,
Yer mommer wouldn't care yet,
But when they was dividin' It
Yer popper wasn't there yet!

Mommer, oo, how good I feel!
Now yer talkin', baby!
Yer mommer sure had sex appeal
An' you have got it, maybe.

Hymn to Science

Science I sing, the Super-Goddess flute,
Evasive Heaven's constant substitute,
For whom the ductless glands distil a soul,
And molecules their zodiacs unroll;
Whom only Fate and common colds escape;
Who lay with Man and so conceived the ape.
Say at the mention of whose mighty name
The phallic spires first drooped with honest shame,
And at whose wall of integrated facts
The human impulse faltered in its acts!
And though the race continues as before
To ride diseases to the further shore,
Who measured the immeasurable void,
And all its dread of darkness thus alloyed?
Who rescued Eros from his brakes and streams
And made him lord of complexes and dreams?
Who traced Suppression to her tangled lair
And found that Love was only safe when bare?
Immortal Science, Queen and Friend of Man,
Successor to Jehovah and His clan,
Who, with a single blast of frigidaire,
Drove from the world the leprosy of·care;
Immortal Science, substituting sense,
Experiment and reason and expense,
For all the hollow shine of dreams and love,
Performed the wonders catalogued above.

Hear then, oh, Maiden, still in rose of youth,
Who found that data were the only truth,
That infinite was finite all in one,
That spots could dare bepox the lordly sun,
And other blessings for our weary days,
Hear then my hail and undiluted praise!
To You, oh, Goddess of Efficiency,
Your happy vassals bend the reverent knee,
Save when arthritis, your benighted foe,
Sulks in the bones and sourly mumbles "No!"
You, only, is my song designed to please,
Though oft the strain is fumbled in a sneeze,
And sneeze succeeding sneeze proclaims, alas!
That Man is still a brother to the ass;
You, only, to whose iron formulae
The patient stars graze tethered in the sky,
Or, waiting till your herdsman Einstein calls,
Stand ringed securely in celestial stalls.

Time was, when in medieval darkness lost,
The frantic race clung to the Holy Ghost,
And brooding in its primitive latrines,
Heard angels singing in its endocrines.
To all the starry host of Heaven they cried,
But had no radio and of course they died:
Each desperate age more wretched than the last—
Some had but poets and of course they passed.
Then You, oh, Science, Super-Muse arose,
And with Promethean pity for our woes,
Stole Saturn's circles from the stormy skies
And placed them neatly under human eyes.
Now loud explosions drown medieval moan;

Men lisp in happy numbers on the 'phone,
And know by name their multitude of germs
Before they yield their bodies to the worms.

Oh, Muse Divine, Hot Mamma of the race,
Whose microscopes can to their secrets trace
All but the whence, the wherefore and the why
Of the immortal foundling of the sky;
Whom only stubborn Destiny evades,
And certain ancient ways of men and maids;
Who rides the whirlwind subway and controls
All animals that lay no claim to souls,
All bugs and beasts of every clime and clan,
Save those that make their habitat in Man,
To whom all earth's phenomena are clear,
Save care, despair, necessity and fear,
Hear then my hail and undiluted praise
For all the other blessings of our days!

A *Lubber Looks at the Sea*

I. *Cliff*

Victorious over 'but' and 'if',
Stands the high, impassive cliff,
As unconcerned with sun or star
As with the bumptious calendar.
The ocean washes every day
A little bit of it away,
And bugs prolific make their home
In its uncouth and tangled dome,
And yet it does not scratch or kick
Or curse the billow or the tick,
Accepting without hope or hurt
The ancient dividends of dirt.
It prods with no complaining mind
The loud and predatory wind,
But hears the dictum of the fates
And placidly disintegrates,
As mindless of Nietzschean balm
As Buddha's over-conscious calm.
It bears the burden of the suns,
Is robbed of slowly-gathered tons,
And swells the unearned increment
Of bandit blasts maleficent—
Yet yields to each his mighty haul
Nor waxes metaphysical,

Nor searches the bewildered sea
For systems of philosophy.
Thus, imperturbable and strong,
No prey to silence or to song,
It baffles with its noble mien
The gods in their perplexed serene,
And juggling neither 'but' nor 'if',
Lives and dies the perfect cliff.

Oh, lyre (I mean the instrument),
Stand by, the while this high intent
I bang upon your bilious strings:
The glory of unquestioning things
I yodel in my febrile fashion;
The mute, immobile lords of passion—
The cliff, the stone, the tree, the sod,
Still hands, that in the lap of God
Lie quietly, while seraphim
And mortals flutter at His whim.
As distant from the hills of joy
As from the glades of *weh* and *oy*,
Midstream in time they stand and are
Bright with the light of every star,
Dark with the dusk of every root
And careless of them all, to boot.
No female of their kind compares
Another's happy lot to theirs,
Or with Icarian wings persuades
Ambition in their neutral shades.
Interdependent, yet alone,
They neither want nor owe nor own,
Nor wonder, while acquiring things,

If planets mumble in their rings,
Nor harry others and themselves
With nonsense from ten thousand shelves,
Whose fecund seed is chiefly sweat,
Whose yield, a heavenly Soviet.

Ah, noble cliff, that gives the sky
An equally Mongolian eye,
By lofty station undismayed,
And of no mystery afraid,
Cast one contemptuous glance on me
Out of your impassivity
Because I hug my 'but' and 'if'
And do not want to be a cliff.

    II. *Shore*

I said, "The sea is lonely, and the sky
Intolerably deep and still and high,
So that the flutter of our upraised hands
Is but a quiver of the wave-worn sands."

I said, "The sun sets always in my mind
And leaves a watch of darkness and of wind
And those unbodied eyes that are the spheres
Upon our dreams, upon our very tears.

"Lay then your near and understanding head
Upon my breast, against the monstrous dead,
For we, the quick, the passing, what have we
In common with the heavens and the sea?"

"How green the sea, how blue the sky!" she said.

I said, "There is laid upon us the weird curse
Of labor with an unborn universe,
And what has our gestation then to do
With ancient green of water or sky-blue?

"Inland upon this island have I seen
The darkness cradle the sun-weary green,
And stars fly low and pin upon the tree
Incongruous fringes of infinity.

"Yet lone the tree stood with its clinging sky,
And lone beneath a wider heaven am I;
For a new chaos cries in us with thirst,
And sea and sky remember but the first.

"For a new chaos cries in us for stars,
And a new order stands beyond the bars,
And ocean mumbling its primordial theme,
Is but the scar of life upon the dream.

"Give me your hand, then; all the rest is old—
The sky is empty and the wave is cold;
The heart has long ago outworn the sea:
Give me your love, and let the sunset be."

"As many worlds as there are eyes," said she.
"Far off the water glooms like dregs of wine,
But here the downs are bathing in the brine.
The moon comes like a lamb upon the sky."

"As many needs as there are hearts," said I.

She said, "The moon is waiting in the sky.
The sea is like a pasture for her mouth.
The dark comes like a shepherd from the south.
The dark climbs like a shepherd north and east.
The foam is like a meadow for her feast.
The downs are waiting for her in the sea.
As many worlds as there are eyes," said she.

"As many worlds as men beneath the sky,
And how shall love bridge all of them?" said I.

"And how may love bridge any of them?" said she,
And saw the sun go down into the sea.

III. *Voyage*

On the other side of the setting sun
I've seen the ashes of things done
And the sand-bars of Avalon.

Peace was there like a white stone;
Peace you could lay your hands upon
And be healed of the hurt of things won.

On the other side of desire I've seen
Stiller than earth, a still demesne,
And colors better than blue or green.

And death walked on the farthest rim,
Horizon-high and friendly and dim,
And all went to confide in him.

And they walked together, the little and large,
In a soundless air by a strange marge
Where time was moored like a spectre-barge.

And far away on the nearer side
There crept a little wounded tide;
And some remembered and some cried.

For that was the world and all its pain;
And that was living and all its gain;
A little cry in a little rain.

Yes, some remembered and some cried,
For note that none of us there had died,
Though the spear was years-long deep in our side.

By our own graves on the grey strands
We sat and warmed our cold hands—
But the hands that we warmed were living hands.

And therefore, some of us heard the tide
Crawl and cry on the nearer side,
And the hands remembered, and some of us cried.

But peace was there like a blessed stone
To lay the remembering hands upon
And the red stigmata of the sun.

And a great healing came thereof,
Of the ashes under, the sky above,
And closed the wounds of life and love.

Spread your sail and bury your mirth,
Your hope and sorrow and dreams and dearth
And your very love in the tight earth,

And sail to the dark of the setting sun,
To the dunes where all things done and won
Heap the pale sands of Avalon.

For there in the dark of desire I've seen
A grey sweeter than blue or green.

There in the dark of desire I've heard
The soft apocalyptic word.

Entr'acte

~~~~~~

I. *Full Fathom Five Thy Father Lies*

(Mr. William Shakespeare's Lyric in Mr. Paul
Whiteman's Tempo.)

Mamma's kind o' lonely;
Mamma's kind o' sad.
Mamma, where is papa?
Mamma, where is dad?

Papa's gone down in his submarine;
Papa's gone after his mermaid queen;
Papa's turned erratic;
Daddy's gone aquatic;
Papa's all wet from base to bean.
Down in the sea-weed with Davy Jones,
Papa is squandering all his bones
On corals and pearls
And bubbles for the diving girls.
Papa is treading the water some;
Oh, what a fish your dad's become!
I'll tell you on the level,
Your daddy was no devil—
There never was a sweller man
Until he did that Kellerman!
Oh, what a change when he comes home!
Won't he look strange with a beaver full of foam,

And his rich alibis
And his fathom five lies!
Watch your mamma tell him what the sea-nymphs
    wouldn't tell;
Watch me give him h - e - double - well,
You can bet
He'll get
His funeral knell,
And his ting-a-ling-a-ting-a-ling-a-ding-dong bell!

    II. *You've Got to See Mamma Every Night or You*
       Can't See Mamma at All

      (Mr. John Millington Synge interprets an American
      theme.)

It's your mamma you'll be looking at seven nights in
the week or not looking at at all, and it's yourself will be
crying and complaining at the sight of her, and crying
and complaining when you'd not be seeing her at all. And
isn't it the hard lot that's fallen on you, what way you
must be choosing and you not knowing which way to
turn. It's a she-devil she is, I'm thinking, that will not be
letting you out one night in the week, and the other
mammas so fine to look at it's the very bones in you do
be crying for a sight of them.

    III. *Mr. William Wordsworth Covers a Human*
      Interest Story for a Tabloid Newspaper

——A simple skirt,
With cocktails on her breath,

Who feels her oats in every limb——
What should she know of death?

I met a little chorus girl,
She was just eighteen, she said;
Her head was thick as many an earl
Who'd clustered round her bed.

She had a town and country air,
And she was barely clad;
Her eyes, you knew, would look so fair
Unto a Pittsburgh lad.

"Husbands and lovers, little maid,
How many may they be?"
"Seven," she answered, unafraid,
And sized up honest me.

"And where are they, I pray you tell."
She answered, "They are seven,
And two of them are gone to Hell,
And two, I think, to Heaven.

"And two of them will never die,
And there is still another,
And in a swell apartment, I
Dwell near him with my mother."

"You say that two are gone to Hell,
And two in Heaven must be;
Yet you are seven—you know damn well,
Sweet wench, you're stringing me."

Then did the little dame reply,
"I tell you they are seven,
And two whose limit was the sky
I hope have gone to Heaven."

"You're stewed, you're stewed, my little maid,
Your voice sounds queer to me;
If four are planted in the shade
Then they are only three."

"Their graves are green and so were they,"
The little jane replied,
"And often with the pearls I play
Which from the boobs I pried.

"These stockings which I now have on,
These pretty rings you see,
The yellow Packard standing yon,
Kind sir, they gave to me.

"And often when I count each bond
And stock, my heart grows sore,
For then my thoughts go out beyond,
And I am sad for more.

"The first that died was Cleveland Jim;
In bed he raving lay,
And when the booze had finished him,
I married Joe that day.

"And after that came Frisco Fred,
Who made his dough in soap;

The next to go was Harvard Ed,
Whose only love was dope.

"Then Mike was in the gravel laid,
In hooch securely soaked."
"How many are they then, sweet maid,
If four of them are croaked?

"If two of them are gone to Hell,
And two, you think, to Heaven,
How many are they, baby?" Well,
She hiccupped and said seven.

IV. *Birdie McReynolds*

    (Mr. Edgar Lee Masters tells an old, old story.)

I kept the house on the corner of Linden and Pine-
    apple Streets,
Down in the district.
And a lively house it was, too,
For a burg like Fork River.
I liked the business,
And that's why I went in it.
Nobody has to do anything he doesn't want to.
How else could I have stuck it out in that hick
    town?
Imagine me a Fork River housewife,
With a Fork River husband,
The kind that used to come down to my house—
Me, Birdie McReynolds!
Don't make me swallow some dirt.

I never lost my virtue.
Don't think it!
I gave it away for a while,
And then I sold it,
And I had a good time both ways.
I knew everybody,
And everybody liked me.
I kept the Judge in his place,
The Mayor, the Sheriff, and the Councilmen,
Or the town couldn't have held them.
They needed somebody like me to tone them down,
The poor, swell-headed, small-town fish,
And it's usually a Birdie McReynolds that does it.
I could read a man's character
By the kind of suspenders he wore;
The old sports went in for white silk ones
With "Fireman" or "Policeman" engraved on the
    buckles.
It made them feel virile,
The poor saps!
Don't think you'll get a sob-story out of me, Eddie
    Masters;
I wasn't that kind of a jezebel.
There ain't any, anyhow.
It's the good women must weep
While the men work.
We like them to work—
They spend more.
Now go away and let me sleep;
That's one thing I never got enough of
In my business,
Or I wouldn't be here.

V. Miss Edna St. Vincent Millay
Goes Wet

I won't get up tomorrow,
Or go to bed tonight,
Unless I know the red wine
Is standing by the white.

Oh, I want the red wine,
And I want the white,
Or I'll sleep with my clothes on
Until I look a sight.

I want to live in Pilsen,
I want to live in Cork,
I want to live anywhere
Except in New York.

I want to live in Paris,
In Munich or in Rome,
With a mouth full of bubbles
And a chin full of foam.

Oh, I want the red wine,
And I want the white,
And I want the dark beer
And I want the light.

Oh, I want to go where drinking
Isn't held a sin;
I want to crush the juniper
Until it is gin.

I'll sail upon the water
Because it isn't dry—
For *I* want the hard stuff,
The Scotch and the rye.

Oh, somewhere east of Suez,
Our best is like their worst,
And it's only a camel
That won't own a thirst.

Oh, to know that I can get it
Whenever I am dry—
The white wine, the red wine,
The Scotch and the rye!

Oh, I could sit a-keening
The rest of the night,
For brandy and sherry
And dark beer and light!

VI. *And Mr. Carl Sandburg, Dry*

Take away the stuff!

Haul it out o' my sight, dump it into the Chicago River,
    clean the streets with it, let the fat-bellied rich wash
    down their frogs' legs with it.

I won't traffic with it; it's poison; it drives you crazy; it
    gives you the D. T.'s and the willies, and I'm not the
    only one that can prove it—

Not by a damsite; not by a long shot; not by the purple
    jowls of the brewers and the distillers—God strike 'em
    dead with their stiff shirts on!

There are ten million wives and widows can prove it; yes,
twenty million; thirty million; thirty-seven million, five
hundred thousand, in the forty-eight States and some
Territories—

And some of the wives have children, and some of the
widows have orphans, all legitimate and registered,
and entitled to decent treatment, and a fine mess
booze has made of them, including those who will
grow up to be Presidents of the United States.

Think of them, forty years from now, sitting in the Blue
Room of the White House, recalling their rotten
childhoods—spoiled and embittered because their fa-
thers came home blind drunk, smelling like a munici-
pal budget, and raised hell and sang drivelling songs,
and fell asleep with their clothes on, anywhere from
the sink to the ceiling—

What kind of Presidents do you think they'll make?

Go among the Hunkies, the Wops, the Micks, the Califor-
nians—the workers and foreigners, who dig the coal
and the ditches and furnish the stuff for the Sunday
rotogravure supplements—

I except the Kikes, who prefer gambling and women—

And you'll see what John Barleycorn has put over; you'll
get your booze-facts straight from the shoulder, so help
me God, you will, I'm telling you till I sweat.

And the same holds for native Americans, as hard-drinking
a race as ever licked their chops in front of a bar, or
in a side-room, or sat down on a curb-stone to wait
for the cop or Xmas.

I hate the stuff.

When you say saloon, I see red buffaloes charging along
the plains like a bloody hurricane;

I want to pull the hair out of my chest, and brandish it
   like a torch in the faces of the anti-prohibitionists, the
   bootleggers, the scofflaws and the big corporations.
Take it out o' my sight; don't tempt me; I wouldn't taste
   it for the stockyards—all right, I'll take a swig, but it
   won't change me, mind; I'm agin it!
Cripes! but I'm agin it!

Apostrophe to a Flea

Nimble and unresting flea,
Do not leap away from me!

Though somewhat different in kind,
We are of a similar mind.

Like yourself, oh, agile flea,
I hop and skip incessantly

From arid here to barren there,
Leaving a zigzag track of air.

Like yourself, I skip and jump
From Life's head to Life's rump,

Scarcely knowing which is which.
I am the flea, the bite, the itch.

Oh, what a destiny we've missed!—
Each a great Industrialist

Leaping with harmonious mind
Upon the earth's immense behind,

The while she sleeps her ancient sleep
And grazes apathetic sheep.

Sometimes in quietness I seem
To hear her scratching in a dream,

With fingers of cool wind and sea,
The bites of multitudinous me—
Her Super-Flea.

Oh, Lesser Insect, you are bound
By lack of Science to the ground,

But we from singing spires shall leap
In aeroplanes upon the deep,

Attack the sylphs who linger there
In the last coverts of the air,

Till they run howling through the blue
And we in roaring swarms pursue.

Oh, Flea, behold us overrun
The purlieus of the shaken sun

And hop and skip and jump and bite
Between the mountains and the light.

The backward aether shall be taught
How sales resistance may be fought,

And mass production shall resound
Tormented leagues above the ground.

The gullies of the moon shall bloom
With a new industrial boom,

And Einstein's void be further bent
To lines of eight and ten per cent.

Oh, what flea-orbits we shall trace
Upon the Universal Face,

While mighty Bankers organize
The vast resources of the skies—

Munition factories in Mars
And tariff rings around the stars.

Oh, nimble and prolific flea,
Lie down and meditate with me
Our slightly different in degree
But common destiny!

The Lover of Verse

The lover of Verse asks very little—
No bitter knowledge his heart depraves—
He is bound to her even by the brittle
Concatenation of the waves.

Foam to him is her white thighs;
Moonlight is her slender hands;
The blue dark is her wide eyes;
He kisses her feet in the sands.

And she, through all disloyalties
Loyal and virgin to each one,
Walks with him in the deep seas,
Rides with him in the sun.

And they are very happy together—
The mad lover at journey's end,
The beautiful woman who is neither
All a mistress nor all a friend:

The proud queen who loved so many,
To all so false, to each so true;
The wise queen who never gave any
Her gift of giving herself anew.

The lover of Verse is simple-hearted
And like a lamb in his delight,
And when the hunters are departed
He walks with the lion in the night;

Walks and talks and is not lonely,
As are the unbelieving wise:
For the multitudinous stars are only
Her two, yet infinite eyes.

He walks, and is not melancholy;
He talks, and bleeds no thorny fears;
For love has turned his lover's folly
To wisdom wiser than the years.

Oh, lover, now the hour is ready,
Bolt the door while love is whole—
The earth is jealous of your body,
The world of your soul!

Summer Day

Better to savor with a reasonable mind
This meat and drink of leaf and light.
Here is the delicate net of Beauty spread on grass,
Caught in the treetops, baited
With the golden, little fishes of the sun.
Let the feet remember, let the heart recall
How once it stored such brightness as this day's
Under the roof of time,
Under the poplar's curd of wind-churned leaves,
Under the apple and the plum trees in the drowsy,
      yellow yard,
Under the feet of darkness.
Let the heart remember how the deciduous days
Withered and fell and made an autumn mound
Upon it. Winter came with gusty candle and a
      spade,
Covered the mound with frost and lamentation,
But dug no grave. For the heart's dead
Are never buried, they arise and walk
But do not come to life.
For the heart's dead arise and walk,
Complain in our completions of their state
With brittle sound of frosty cerements,
But will not live again.

251

Oh, let the heart ensnared, not fall among these
   dead!

Even now, Autumn, with cupped ear, listens to the
   night-long cricket voices,
Following by the crinkled stars, camping by suns
   not far away.
Even now, Winter walks after, slowly, with nimbus
   of pale, polar light,
Dry branch for stave, scrip full of frozen roots,
Gathering wan ends of days for fuel for his crackling
   stars.

Oh, let the heart, ensnared, not fall upon this brightness!

Better walk warily where the trap is spread;
Let the eyes remember, that persuade the soul,
Colors and compositions of delight,
The falling days, the frost, the long darkness
   mournful,
The dead who walk complaining in our joys.
Oh, let the eyes remember, the ears hear again
Under the mound, under the dusty days that crackle
   no more,
Where the burning shards of the broken spears and
   helmets of the sun
Lie cooled and rusted in the darkness under the
   ferns,
Let the eyes and ears remember, and the heart,
Grasses like this, quickened to fragrance under the
   wind's blue horn,

This blown gold winnowed to glassy clearness,
This diminutive sea-music in the leaves,
This quail whistling out of the perfection of his
     place,
These glints of the broken spears and helmets of the
     sun
Under plumed boughs,
This white horse in the field behind the trees,
With legless motion swimming in the sun above the
     green,
Like one of Neptune's horses in the wave,
Flecked and striped with green water,
These white gashes of the wind-blade in the sea's
     blue mail,
Flashing crystals of foam on the cobalt sea
Beyond the distant cliff-edge. . . .

                                    Then the day
Changing with delicate desire after the wind's too-
     rude embrace;
Changing with delicate thirst, a bowl of yellow air,
     gathering raindrops;
Trees yellow in wet glass, meadows and hills
In vitreous yellow shimmering.

These were, became a shape, running and dancing,
     with golden, gossamer wingspread;
The heart followed, through the cities and the sor-
     rows, over the downs, to the cliff-edge,
Over the sea, to the wine-red sea-line, through doors
     of green and gold,
Studded with bright, new stars . . . out of the world.

253

Even now, the newly-buried startle up to awful
    recognition,
Beginning the last of all their many deaths,
Beginning their everlasting sojourn with the dead,
Stare at the monstrous dark with drooping paws up-
    reared,
Standing in eternal indecision,
The silence dribbling from its shapeless jaws,
And receive the blessing of the apostolic worm. . . .

These too, followed over the sea to the wine-red sea-
    line,
Through doors of green and gold studded with
    bright new stars . . .
To this place.
Even now, Autumn, with cupped ear, listens to the
    night-long cricket voices . . .
Winter walks after.

But even before Autumn spreads her household goods
    in the trees,
And the pale warriors of the polar sun
Camp in the orchard, grazing their wild horses
Under the pear trees, by the cold, stone fence on the
    hill,
The sun will slope to the west, into the frigid
    sea,
Sea, slow-moving, like a great, grey turtle, plated
    and ridged by wind and cold,
Pitted with desolation like the moon,
Pawing the feet of cliffs;

The massed gulls of the night swoop down upon the
    crumbs of light;
The wind stumble and howl in darkness,
Like a primordial beast with fumbling pads
Lost in the new, fixed order of the hills,
Of land and water, day and night;
The heart, too, will slope westward after its knowl-
    edge, into the frigid sea,
Pitted with desolation like the moon,
Pawing at rock;
The burning shards of the sun cool in the grass;
The trumpet-flower and the quail be stilled of their
    color and their cry,
And a new shape of sorrow and of loss
Stand in the dooryard, translucent, under the sad,
    cold stars.

                                For all that stays
Forever, after the green and golden doors are closed,
And the shape is gone from the cities and the cliffs,
And the darkness gathers the net of Beauty in the
    grass,
Is the beast, earth-bound, claws clipped, tail twisted
    and forlorn,
Lost in the old, fixed order of the hills,
Forest and field and day and night,
Fumbling his nude, weak cities with lewd and un-
    familiar hands,
Crying in quails his own faint, scarce-remembered
    cry of place,
Fretting, struggling, feeding, breeding,
Flea-bitten by a soul.

As the Crow Flies, Let Him Fly—Poems Containing Mottoes for Wall or Desk, Moral Precepts, and Other Instructive and Diverting Matters, So Expressed, That He Who Runs May Run (If He Likes)

I

She walks in beauty, like the night,
And so she should, the parasite!

II

The cat sits;
The bat flits—
The nit-wits!

III

The camel isn't very bright,
In spite of his amazing height,
And so obeys the greater guile
Of creatures he could kick a mile.

IV

Behold the High Official, he
Is gazing at the Treasury.
He wears an inward-looking smile,
His cheerful face is full of guile;

256

He loves the people and their cause,
Their shining faces and applause.
He'd die for dear Democracy,
And lives but for the Treasury.

V

Sing a song of sixpence,
And sing it till you die;
And this I'll bet, you'll never get
A pocketful of rye.

VI. *To an Altered Cat*

Unaware of sun or moon,
Indifferent to bane or boon,
He stares at nothingness, content
Without his feline complement.

No passion animates his pose;
No memories his eyes disclose;
The loveliest female of his kind
Leaves not a shadow on his mind.

He takes his liver and his beef,
As we the glory and the grief;
Then, having eaten, he surveys
Our gloomy struggle with the days.

Ah, more serene than carven stone,
Victorious over mirth and moan,
He lolls upon the couch, to wait
The dust for which we war with fate.

Ah, you who pity Thomas, say,
Do you, like him, possess your day?
He tempers to the shears the wind,
Who alters to his doom his mind.

VII

Fools may go
Where angels wouldn't;
But then, we know,
The angels couldn't;
If angels could, I think they'd try
A little folly on the fly.

VIII

If you're a naughty little girl,
The least you'll get will be an earl;
Sin must prosper, or it's bored,
While virtue is its own reward.

IX

I understand that God is not
Confined to any sphere or spot,
But roams, in this or that disguise,
Through Paris, as through Paradise.
He's here and there and everywhere,
Above, below, and in the air,
And may with certainty be found,
The prophets tell us, on the ground.
I do not doubt that this is so:
I take the word of those who know,
And yet, I sometimes wonder why
The steeples point Him in the sky,

And not a single church makes clear
That He may be as often here.

X

I envy things of wood or stone
Beyond the reach of mirth and moan,
That neither greed nor grief nor sex
Nor Jove nor Juno's self can vex.
They lose their hour of jazz, 'tis true,
A joke, a love affair or two,
But on the other hand they miss
What counter-irritants of bliss!
Often would I myself deny
My three-inch sight of city sky,
The junk that clutters up my mind,
The dubious comfort of my kind,
The surreptitious beer and gin
And all the sour fruit of sin,
If I could only sit and stare
Like silly pictures on the air.
How much we pay to say, "*Je suis*,"
"*Ich bin*," or "*Sum*," or even "*Me*"!

XI

A bird in the hand may sometimes be
Worth a couple in a tree;
That depends upon the kind
Of bird you caught and had in mind.
A lark in air is worth, I think,
Twenty sparrows in a sink,
And I should rather see birds fly
Than find them singing in a pie.

259

XII

Fish have scales but cannot sing
Or play the flute or anything,
While never yet the goat was born
That blew a tune upon his horn.
If I were made like fish or goats,
You may be sure I'd meet my notes.

XIII

Well may he be to censure blind,
Who is found charming by his kind.

XIV

The early bird may catch the worm;
I do not care for foods that squirm;
I'll wait till noon to make my rounds,
And catch some coffee off the grounds.

XV

I'm not a huntsman bold and brave;
I'd surely run my skin to save;
If I encountered bull or bear,
I'd lose, if not my pants, my hair;
A tiger burning fairly bright
Would kill me seven times with fright.
Faint hearts as palpitant as mine,
Must battle with the dandelion.

XVI

It took much longer than a day
To build a town like Rome, they say;

Yet now, the mightiest thing in Rome
Is Mussolini's storied dome:
It's not how long it took, but how
It took at all, that milks the cow.

XVII

The lion roars, the echoes try
To simulate that lordly cry;
But having said their little say,
The echoes quickly fade away.

Pass, Oh, Time

~~~~~~~~~~~~~~~~~~~~~~~~~~~~~~~~~~~~~~

Pass, oh, Time (oh, Passing Medicinal)
pass in the rustling of trees,
in the clarity of this light,
over the crystal, smooth floor of the sun,
over the golden grass.
As dew in the night to the leaf,
as rain to the seed
is your going unto me.
Oh, Passing Medicinal,
oh, apple ripened in the fragrant wood,
oh, Song Completed, Life Resolved,
Pain ripened, withered, fallen into dust,
Desire shored, as the breakers are shored
and at rest in the sand
that quenches the bite of the salt in their
        throats,
under the aegis of your viewless wings
I walk through the whirlwind,
I walk through my doom.
In the tent of your wing-spread I wait,
till the clash of the sabres is stilled,
and riders and horses thin out
into air, as a vapor, a dream,
and the tent and the desert and fear
together dissolve into darkness.

And even these who labor in the sun,
hewing down trees in the orchard,
unmindful of you,
shall meet you with arms full of branches,
lie down in silence sweeter than their leaves,
in fragrance of all flowers that ever grew,
in orchards blowing with the branchèd stars.

～～～～～～～～～～～～～～～～～～～

I. *Moonlight in the Street*

It lies like tired, spent lightning, that has fallen
      asleep on the ground;
It melts the cold dark into music, into music that
      breathes not a sound;
It sheets the dead trees in splendor, with motherly
      fingers and kind,
And it eases soft as a carpet, the stinging feet of
      the wind.

It is Beauty reft of its passion; it is Pathos
      cleansed of its pain;
It is spun of the veins of lilies, and of sun-threads
      sunken in rain;
It is born of the Darkness praying, with a Dawn-
      light on her face,
And the Ultimate Pity has sent it, a grace of Her
      Grace.

II. *Rest from Desire*

The years shall bring us rest
From wind and fire;
But sweetest still and best,
Rest from desire.

264

For Sorrow trudges by,
And tears are dry
In the light o' the sun;
But the heart's unwearied spinning
Is never, never done,
From Life's strange, sad beginning,
Till the grave is won.

We shall rest in the silent sea
From storm and wind and fire;
But the sweetest rest shall be
Rest from desire.

III. *Crape on the Door*

The dead they sleep a long, long sleep;
The dead they rest, and their rest is deep;
The dead have peace, but the living weep.

The moonlight sleeps like a silver lake . . .
The dead they know nor pain nor ache;
The living watch, and their hearts they break.

The night stands mute at the shuttered pane . . .
The dead shall need no prayers again,
But the living cry unto God in vain.

The wind goes by with a weary moan . . .
The dead lie stark and still as stone,
But the hearts of the living cry for their own.

The candles gleam where the pale dead sleep . . .
The dead they rest, and their rest is deep;
The dead have peace, but the living weep.

The dead they sleep—and soft is their bed.
Oh, why do the living weep for the dead?
And why not weep for themselves instead?

IV. *Memorial*

My mother walked where I walked;
She held me by the hand;
But her eyes were walking elsewhere
In a sad, blue land.

Plums fell in the stillness;
Leaves grieved in the wind;
But another day was shining
In my mother's mind.

The summer lay in the garden
And suckled the breasts o' the sun;
But my mother had forgotten
That other summers were done.

Alien in the garden,
Exile under the sun,
My mother had forgotten
That her youth was done.

My mother and I walked slowly;
She held me by the hand;

But I heard the leaves in the garden,
And she in another land.

I heard the leaves in the garden
Grieve in the summer wind;
But the sorrow that grew in Zion
Grieved in my mother's mind.

The plums dropped beside her;
My mother did not start;
For the shadow that rose in Russia
Sighed in my mother's heart.

The sorrow that grew in Zion,
My mother under the tree,
And the shadow that rose in Russia
Sighed like the severing sea—

The sea, whose arm is mighty;
The sea, whose wrath is blind,
That scatters the sons of Israel
Like leaves upon the wind—

That scatters the sons of Israel
Until His Will is done,
Alien in their gardens,
Exiles under the sun.

The eyes that look on sorrow
Look not upon the sun:
My mother had forgotten
That her youth was done.

Leaves fell in the garden
And brushed my mother's face;
But my mother walked with her mother
In a distant time and place.

My mother stood where I stood,
And held me by the hand;
But I knew my mother was little
In another land.

V. *Out of Your Littleness*

Out of your littleness, out of your slightness,
A world I shape me, sturdy and strong;
Out of your stillness, out of your whiteness,
Radiance and song.

I need no opiate out of the heavens,
Nor wine of the vine of the valley or steep;
You are my nectar and nepenthe,
Battle and sleep.

I need not follow the great clouds sailing
Swan-wise to the Hesperides;
Or sun or moon, that renew their failing
Strength in the seas.

You are the fruit of the golden garden;
You are the silver swans in the skies;
I am renewed with the love that rises
Out of your eyes.

Like tired birds, my sorrows flutter
Out of the east and out of the west;
Descend and find, my love, what utter
Peace on your breast!

VI. *Admonition*

Hear you, all you celibate,
Who take Heaven for a mate,
Has no warning from above
Told you Death can also love?

Loving you, he'll draw his sword
And fight for you against your Lord,
Slay Him in some graveyard gloom
And wed you in his narrow room.

VII. *When I Was Little*

When I was little I used to sit
In the kitchen by the stove;
Like candle-shades my thoughts would flit,
Nor from those four walls ever rove.

Blue and red the tumbled coals
Made a witches' wood of fire;
The wind with league-long fingers struck
Anger from his iron lyre.

Winter huddled like a beast
Round the house in icy fur,

As he waited for a feast
On the first that dared to stir.

Through the window I saw the stars,
Frozen orphans of the skies,
Watery with pain of cold
As if they were poor human eyes.

And behind, I seemed to see
God in regnant posture tense,
Buttoned snugly to His beard
In His own magnificence.

Lord of all the prophets He,
To the pious visible,
Holding Moses on His knee,
Looking down on Israel.

Patriarch of Patriarchs,
Only friend of Israel,
Gazing on this very room;
For my mother knew Him well.

Silently my mother went
Through the kitchen, by the stove,
Heaping warm against the dawn
Little services of love.

Singing half and sighing half,
What she did I never knew,
For the served are unaware
What the servant finds to do.

From Lithuania my mother came,
Half a mother, half a child;
The long and bitter sea that brought,
Sweetly home her heart beguiled.

Sweet and sad her heart beguiled;
The mother toiled; the maiden yearned—
Her face was like a shaded lamp
That softly screened the soul that burned.

Sitting wistful by the stove,
I felt her dream uneasily;
I saw her mother in the coals
Wave her heart away to sea.

My mother's heart did weep in mine;
We were two children in my breast;
My sorrow took my mother's shape
And soothed me tenderly to rest.

So by my sorrow comforted,
Nodding in the candle-light,
I followed it upstairs to bed
And left my mother to the night.

VIII. *Sing, Wind of Summer!*

Sing, wind of summer, through the leaves;
You are not all that grieves,
Seeking some golden thing that has no name
In your melodious winging
Beneath the cloudy moon,

271

I hear my own heart singing
As sad, as lorn a tune,
Pursuing vain, like you, some trackless flame,
Forever wandering,
Of love, of joy, of fame.
Sing, wind of summer, sing!
Sing!

IX. *Remonstrance*

Let the tears be dry in your eyes, and the cloud melt
on your brow;
The dead were crying once as you are crying now;
They were crying in the deserts; they were crying
by the streams;
They cried out in their waking, and they cried aloud
in their dreams;
The cities were full of their clamor; the walls
leaned over their moan—
Can you hear so much as a sigh now, under the
heavy stone?

There will be maidens like you and young men
younger than I;
They will watch the fiery shoots of the spring spread
over the sky;
They will sing their songs to each other; they will
kiss and deceive;
They will be crying, too, for all living things must
grieve;
And we shall seem as foolish to them finding a reason
for tears,

272

As they seem foolish to us now, who are dead a
thousand years.

There was a young girl like you once, in Carthage
or Tyre or Troy,
Who wept through her hair till midnight because of
a roving boy;
There was a young man like me once, in Egypt or
Rome or Greece,
Who hunted an ancient heartache, and called it the
golden fleece:
Is there any could now imagine the greatness and
gulf of their grief?
Would you smile if you looked for their story under
that fallen leaf?

Time is a drunken High-Priest, to whom it is sin to
weep;
He tramples the grief of Jacob along with his sire's
sheep;
The things of dust are his hunger; the tears of men
are his thirst;
Let him go parched for the second; let him take
grass for the first.
So dry the spring in your eyes then, and drive the
cloud from your brow,
And laugh as you look for your story a hundred
years from now.

X. *Words*

Under my words securely lie
How many passions born to die,

How many moments poised for flight
Upon a ledge of day or night.

And yet the work was not amiss,
Was not in vain, in spite of this.
(I aimed at no Acropolis.)

For in the striving, lo, I found
Silence with a starry sound,
A green tree in a singing wood,
A happy host in solitude,
Jesus jesting merrily
With a lad in Galilee,
Who, therefore, through his life's whole span
Loved the Saviour for the Man.

And in the striving, lo, I heard
A new moon warbling like a bird,
A new moon laughing like a child
Because it was by space beguiled.

And in the striving, lo, I saw
Love break the brutal sword of Law.
Still from sky-roof and strange sea-floor
The everlasting spirits cry
For men to live before they die.

And still a million hearts reply,
And pound upon the granite door
With love and drink and dreams and fears
And desperate anger of the years.

And some there are who even try
Above the mountainous wall to fly,
Like foolish birds
With little, broken wings of words.

Apologia

Though I made songs clear as green-housed birds,
Or bells going their Sabbath round,
Or the wind driving the silver nails
Of summer rain into the ground;

Though I made songs as high and shining
As stars fleeing their storm-barred jails,
Or the moon shaking her dripping horns
After the charge of the tempest fails;

Though I made songs as strange and witch-like
As cloud-ships sailing leisurely
The burning inlets of the sundown
With cargoes from the crimson sea;

Though I made songs as wise and placid
As the look in a dead man's face,
Where the still flood of the fatal lightning
Lies like a dawn in a desert place;

Greater than all my songs am I;
Much more have seen, have heard much more—
For who shall fetch in a pitcher of singing
All that lies on the ocean-floor?

Who shall fetch in a cruse of verses
All that lies on the mind's sea-floor,
Or lift on the point of a sword of song
All that lies at the heart's deep core?

Though the pitcher be cunningly carven as hope,
Though the sword be sharp as the blade of truth—
Holds Death a half of a life-time of dying?
Holds Life a tenth of the thoughts of youth?

Though I made songs lovely as love surrendered,
Though I made songs wise as an empty skull,
The fields of the mind must rot with harvest,
The sea of the heart be ever full.

Pencil in the Air

Proem

~~~~~~~~~~~~~~~~~~~~~~~~~~~~~~~~~~~~~

Wherever I go,
I go too,
And spoil everything.

Children's Album

~~~~~~

I. *History*

Besides the Lord's mysterious love,
History is a record of
The long attempt
Of Church and State
To exterminate,
Eradicate,
Extinguish and obliterate,
Expunge, annul, annihilate,
Demolish, quell and abrogate,
Dismantle, ruin and efface,
Squelch and scuttle without trace
The human race
By war and fire and rope and ax,
Wheel and water, dungeon, tax,
Hunger, terror, torment, wrong,
Despair and serfdom, thirst and thong.

To which, so runs the document,
The victim gave complete assent,
And thought
And sought
And wrought
And fought

Fiercely to co-operate
And handsomely participate!

Well, since they strive that this befall,
I wish success to one and all,
And know, when Church and State alone
Stand naked stone to naked stone,
The beasts and birds and crawling things
Will leave the proper offerings.

II. *Budget*

The gonad is designed to mate us,
And thereby, obviously, create us,
Whereas the mute, minute bacillus
Is admirably made to kill us:
A balanced budget in this case
Would greatly benefit the race.

III. *Experience*

The weirdest ills are put to rout
By having teeth and tonsils out,
But if, with teeth and tonsils banished,
The ills referred to have not vanished,
It is generally understood
The operation did no good.

IV. *Birds*

An ostrich on his native sand
Is worth a couple in the hand;

283

The same is applicable to
The minatory marabou,
Although the proverb may insist
A bird is worth more in the fist.

V. *The Saddle*

Capital, Labor, Rich or Poor,
Rightist, Leftist, East or West,
Death and taxes and this are sure—
Who sits in the saddle rides herd on the rest.

Cross or Crescent, Dragon or Sickle,
Brawn or Brains or Stricken or Blest—
The Hand that turns the wheel is fickle:
Who sits in the saddle rides herd on the rest.

Sadist or Saviour, Layman, Priest,
The Devil-damned or the God-possessed—
The feast of Power is a heady feast:
Who sits in the saddle rides herd on the rest.

The few or the many, the Right or Wrong,
The Justice-driven, the Hate-confessed—
The song of Power is a siren song:
Who sits in the saddle rides herd on the rest.

Fellow creature and desperate foe,
Death is a terror, so live we must,
But this is a truth we hide and know—
We sit in the saddle or lie in the dust.

284

VI. *A Little (Not Much) about the Ladies*

Women have three years to hope in;
The fourth, they leap into the open,
And hence, by masculine acclaim,
Leap year gets its name and fame,
Although, with subtle skill in mating,
They pull some fast ones, too, while waiting.

VII. *Fifth Commandment*

Love your parents, not as such,
But since like you, forlorn,
They too began this life in dutch,
Not asking to be born.

VIII. *The Oceans*

The oceans, like necrophilists,
Paw dead shores and breed dead mists;
The mineral eyes of darkness stare
As blind as bats on barren air—
Thus do the seas and stars equip
The studious mind for statesmanship.

IX. *Cradle Song*

Fear not the atom in fission;
The cradle will outwit the hearse;
Man on this earth has a mission—
To survive and go on getting worse.

X. *Geopolitics*

Birds live in air and fish in water,
Somebody's son in somebody's daughter,
The tasseled corn in corn fritters,
The caterpillar on front-porch sitters,
Americans, in ice-cold cokes,
The farmer's daughter in watchfob jokes,
Good intentions in obvious louses,
Tillamook deaths in doomèd mouses,
Tergiversations, equivocations,
In the relations between nations,
Anfractuosities in harried
Loving couples legally married,
Termites in rented, high-priced homes,
Nonsense and blight in holy domes,
Massed men and women in headline hordes,
Statesmen in hand-sprayed vocal chords,
Pigs in clover and clover in pigs,
Adult folk in bent twigs,
Illusions, when the blossoms fall,
In jury-duty and alcohol,
The sound scratch in the sound itch,
And sainthood in the stony niche.

Most of us live, with troubled breath,
In hope of dying a painless death.

XI. *From the Chinese*

No taxee—no lendee—
No gottee—no spendee.

XII. *Effect of Humans on Animals, on the Universe and on the Author*

1. ON ANIMALS

The antics of the human race
Bespectacle the house-fly's face,
Who peers bemused at me and you
And dives bewildered into glue;
The hare essays in vague unease
Continuous carnalities,
And nibbles, while his ear observes,
Lettuce for his jumpy nerves;
The termite, cowering with the mouse,
Runs amok, brings down the house;
The headlines scampering through his head,
The goat becomes more capriped,
Disdains the tin can on his table
Because he dreads the printed label;
The horse instinctively inveighs
Against you with emphatic neighs;
The zany lion in the zoo
Attempts a roar, achieves a moo;
Fish, large and small, in fronded seas,
Stare at your Bikinanities,
Your spin-the-top uncertainties
At silly water weirdly hurled,
And think the mushroom is the world;
Even the dog, whom Nature meant
To be at ease and reticent,
Tries his confusion to dispel
With baffled barks of doggerel,

And, Nightmare's neurasthenic own,
Gnaws for the answer at a bone.

2. ON THE UNIVERSE AND ON THE AUTHOR

Two billion people, black and white,
Bi-sexual, male, and parasite,
Dismay the earth, astound the sea,
Bewilder Death and chisel me!

XIII. *Statesman*

Sired by Narcissus, Demos-damm'd, he stands
And primps for history before the herd,
The rabbit of salvation in his hands
Extracted from the empty, silken word,

Or, like the pigeons in the pepper trees,
Perched on his high confusions, drearily
Regurgitating rancid elegies,
Drops nostrums on the demagogracy.

Madrigal Macabre

Some want a vault, some want a grave,
Bold sailors the sepulchral wave;
To some cold lives it has hotly mattered
That they be burned and their ashes scattered;
Some souls bemused with fear of haunts
Want to be buried beside their aunts;
Most urban jokers, treys and deuces
Want to be laid under hometown spruces;
Pharaohs stanch and Pharaohs fickle
Agreed upon a permanent pickle,
Surrounded by such lesser dills
As needful to their royal wills;
Some want a headstone, some a slab,
Some flowers, some rice—as good, but drab;
Some want a funeral de luxe,
Some specify but dogs and cooks;
Some want violent lamentation,
Some a muted murmuration;
Some wills grow jolly and complete
With wakes and hot, baked funeral meat,
With women keening and men drinking
And the corpse, as it imagines, winking;
Some want show and some deceases
Want neither choir nor Rest-in-Peaces;
Some, dying, feel their own tears flow
At thought of a pal saying, "Good old Joe!";

Some will not close a final eye
Until assured their graves are dry;
Some who know gardens and manure
Are partial to damp sepulture;
Some would like the works entire,
Burial, mausoleum, pyre,
The gloved cortege, the plumèd horse,
The lodges out in splendid force—
But I, who have but thinly thrived,
Should much prefer to be revived.

Desert Song

After the trouble and the tears,
After the wraths and the wraiths depart,
Peace, nurtured by the lonely years,
Blooms like a cactus in the heart

And pierces all—what dreams, what truth,
What hopes and joys yet dare to keep
The vigil of remembered youth,
Until they gently bleed to sleep.

The Grail

Together we have learned, where nettles grow;
Where not the vanished, but the living sup,
What Galahad, enchanted, did not know:
The Grail is in the seeking, not the Cup.

Autobiography with Adjuration
or
Emergency Measure
or
O Congress, Give the Children Beer

Now sinks the sun (and so do I—
And what does not?) and in the sky
The stars like little lambs appear
And baa to the poetic ear,
While I, reduced by sundry woes
To tweedy verse and tattered prose,
Survey, like the insensate sod,
The grand, nocturnal style of God,
As deaf, as blind, when Beauty calls,
As if I were Niagara Falls.

So what? So then, I stand and stare
Upon the buildings and the air
And wonder, in the global gloom,
Why men create, then damn their doom;
Why simple meanings of the world,
Like flags of fallen armies furled,
Lie on the shelves of little minds
While Chaos her own flag unwinds;
Why failing faiths and feet should tread
The huge synopsis of the dead;
Why they who hew or heal or pull

Be empty when the earth is full;
Why bloodiest war could not make taut
The texture of the common thought;
Until at last I take to bed
The clamant sparrows in my head
And count, amid the jeers of Sleep,
What's left to count? the tax on sheep,
A goat or two, confined in banks,
For transfer to the income blanks.

So then? (Oh, let a fellow rhyme
Some small diversion out of Time!)
So then—O bardlings, go and bait your
Need of joy with dreams of Nature—
With honey-hauling, solvent bees;
With reeds and roses, rain and trees
And birds who stir their leaves with song,
As cuckoo as the day is long,
Or those who owl throughout the night
Their avian dirges of delight;
With sun and shade and stream and lake
And wood—and give yourselves a brake!
But not for me, when times appal,
The whippoorwill and waterfall,
Cathartic palm or unguent pine—
Another subterfuge is mine
When the volcanic days require
A quick hegira from the fire,
And Thought, in undershirt and pants,
Must flee the Furies and Finance—
For then, in wistful dream, I fly
Hot-foot before the doleful I

And find (O beatific boon!)
A refuge in the old Saloon!
O happy shelter, hallow'd cove,
The heart's deflated treasure-trove,
The gentle Growler's mirror'd cave,
Home of the hopped and malted brave,
Not of the rapture and the rest
You poured into the adult breast
I mumble on my cracked bassoon,
But of my childhood joys, Saloon,
When as a tot I tottered in
And with an upward-pointing chin,
As needle to the northern star,
Was magnetized unto the bar!
There, like a mariner inspired,
By Davil Sea to frenzy fired,
I stood upon the rail, surveyed
The billowing schooner unafraid,
Disdained the alien corn, and home
Plunged into the siren foam.
O plushy foam, O hurricane blow,
O splash upon the floor below
Around the inviolate spittoon;
O squadron gait, O triple moon
Revealed above the swinging door
(O triple crescent, sometimes four),
O nubile hiccup, meek and mild,
Confessing the transported child,
That like a frightened mouse would start
And melt to love the hardest heart;
O infant playmates gathered round
A foot above the sawdust ground,

Who shared the pleasures fierce and fine
Of goblet, schooner, tankard, stein,
Or piped with me what tender tunes
Comprise the saga of saloons,
When, in the advancing summer night,
The men from pits of anthracite
Tramped thunderous through the yielding door
And bought us all a round or more,
While other boys were killing frogs,
Or tying cans to orphan dogs,
Or trampling on the lettuce-beds,
Or breaking windows, doors, and heads,
Or stealing milk and copper wire,
Or setting outhouses on fire,
Or making gentle faces blanch
Of pious Christians (Hebrew branch),
Or tearing linen from the line,
Or filching gadgets from the mine,
Or swiping marbles from the meeker,
Or punching noses of the weaker,
And learning all the paltry tricks
Of trade, finance, and politics—
O playmates of a halcyon day,
What verse (I ask you) could convey
The innocent, the clean, the clear,
The golden comradeship of beer,
When, harmless as a day in June,
We quaffed it in the old saloon?
Stay down, O sad and sunken sun,
While Echo sourly grumbles, "None!"

For children bred in a saloon
Are harmless as a night in June,
And when to Man's estate they grow,
Retain the vernal *status quo*.
They never learn the tawdry tricks
Of trade, finance, or politics,
Or harbor sinister intent
Of one day being President,
Or Congressman, or Senator,
Ambassador or Governor,
Or Universal Financiers,
Or Other-People's Budgeteers—
But simple as the sunny grass,
They let the cycles come and pass
And sometimes mewingly rehearse
The tricks of tetrametric verse,
Or daub a ship in morning light,
Or mine a bit of anthracite,
Or sit on curbs in urban byways
Or fences on bucolic highways,
Or by romantic melancholy
Freed early from all earthly folly,
Lie peacefully and stare at rain
And tickle roots up into grain.

O Congress, as you hold them dear,
Give the hapless children beer;
Restore their gentle nurse, Saloon,
To keep them simple and immune
From every influence that shapes

Young manhood into adult apes;
From mousy mayhems, cheap assaults,
And other small, felonious faults;
Transmute into a public good
Their picayune delinquenthood,
Their piddling pilfering of cars,
And make them noble men in bars—
If they must show their manhood clear,
Let them knock off the heads of beer,
That to their pristine natures true,
They may not grow to be like you;
Oh, save them from the sallow yield
Of church and school and playing field,
Where (*vide* Duke of Wellington)
Such bays as Waterloo are won,
And the alternate brag and whine
Are neatly tuned to rain and shine,
And, as you hold the future dear,
O Congress, give the children beer!

Progress

~~~~~~

They'll soon be flying to Mars, I hear—
But how do you open a bottle of beer?

A flash will take you from Nome to New York—
But how the hell do you pull a cork?

They'll rocketeer you to Hibernia—
But open a window and get a hernia.

They've stripped space from the widow'd blue—
But where is the lace that fits a shoe?

Where is the key that fits a lock?
Where is the garter that holds a sock?

They'll hop to the moon and skip to the stars,
But what'll stay put are the lids on jars.

The mighty telescope looks far,
But finds no place to park a car.

The world crackles with cosmic minds
Tangled up in Venetian blinds.

One day they'll resurrect the dead,
Who'll die again of colds in the head.

Nocturne: West Los Angeles

Faintly tremulous, the night
Exudes her mild and membranous light,
And on the garden's flowery floor
The cat inhales the sycamore,
Sprawls on the parsley, mint or chives,
Felicitous in all his lives,
Or from a comfortable ledge
Views the horizon of a hedge,
Alert, assured, compact, complete,
Poised for aggression or retreat,
Unlicked, save by his own caress
In the neat cause of cleanliness,
At one with all, at peace, at ease
In all his fine felinities—
Surely along some scented sod
He ate that scurrying mouse called God.

Demos Is Done

Demos is done, the brute that ruled too long,
Spewed tyrants, tended them and made them strong,
Crushed God and good, blocked wisdom's gentle ways,
Spat at the sunrise of evolving days,
Clubbed Truth, made compact with the ancient dead,
That he be safely chained and poorly fed.
Aristos comes to take him by the hand
And weeping Demos waits the mild command,
The roomier collar, bigger bone, clean floor,
The window'd kennel and the sky-blue door.

Flies Without Ointment

I. *I'm Fond of Doctors*

I'm fond of doctors and drivers of hacks
Whose names are Morris and Barney and Max;
I'm fond of waiters in places I know
Whose names are Louis and Mike and Joe;
They take my mind off taxes and love—
A very good taking the mind off of.

II. *Good Morning,*
Browning

God's in his heaven
Painting things blue;
I'm on the thorn,
The snail is too.

III. *Oral History and*
Prognostication

One cannot mastic-
Ate with plastic;
Porcelain stains;
Cement pains;
Gold glitters;

302

Diamond twitters;
Lead sinks;
Iron stinks;
Wood rots;
Coal blots;
Zinc corrodes;
Uranium explodes;
Bridges miss;
Plates hiss;
Copper hums—
Hurrah, gums!

IV. *When I Peruse the Journals*

When I peruse the journals gray with strife
On earth, and hence assume distress above,
I must conclude, regretfully, that life
Seems (no reflection on the honest wife)
The occupational disease of love.

V. A *Couple of Dachshunds*

A couple of dachshunds are Sweeney and Joe,
As pleasant companions as any I know;
Their persons are decent, though slightly mephitic;
Their ancestry German, their noses Semitic.
Their appetites frankly are rather Teutonic—
Gargantuan, colossal, immense, mastodonic,
But whatever the faults of the children of Moses,
I am glad that the rest of them followed their noses.

VI. *To the Human Rump*

Disparaged and derided part,
Disdained by manners, morals, art,
What change in stricken Man's estate
If only you endured its weight—

If hands and head were cast aside,
The claws of greed, the spring of pride,
And till there was no more Begat,
The world sat down and sat and sat!

VII. *The Mockingbird*

The mockingbird sings in the sycamore tree,
The poplar, the lemon, the willow;
His coloratura exacerbates me
As I pound my anfractuous pillow.

I harbor no prejudice, nourish no gall
For occasional bird singing sweetly,
But exiguous mocking of nothing at all—
I can do that myself, and more neatly.

My sleep is compounded of nightmare and rue;
I toss like a boat on a billow—
Alas, I regret there is nothing to do
But report him to Caesar Petrillo.

VIII. *Famous Battle*

My lady is lovely as iris or rose,
Or blossom of apple or cherry;

My feeling for her from her head to her toes
Is floriverous, fancy, and very.

And yet I regret to confess a distress
I repress when I can, lest it strike her—
My lovely and lissome and lyrical, yes,
I love her—but really don't *like* her!

IX. *Sad, Mad Song*

Love flies out of the window
When I come in through the door;
When I come in through the window,
Reverse, and pour—
So, partly serious, but more in jes',
I try to find rhymes for oranges.

X. *Shepherd Song: 1947*

From womb to worm and worm to weed
What does a person really need?—
A million for food and clothes and rent;
A billion for innocent merriment;
A trillion to balance the budget and
A zillion for taxes, to keep on hand;
A zillion more, and the hillside's dew-pearled,
And what do you think we've got?—One World!
And one can live as cheaply as two—
So what is there really for you to do
But draw the curtain and go to bed
And pull the cover over your head

305

And lie there warm and well-concealed
And consider the lilies of the field?
Man wants so little here below:
The items listed—the rest is show.

Revelation

In the Evening

Star-bright in the evening,
The apricot blossoms seem to sing,
Sing to the harassed heart and mind
Something infinitely kind,
Something compassionate. I strain
To hear the numbers mild as rain,
To see the sweet tree's flower-kissed
Beneficent evangelist;
And then a word is murmured clear,
Then two, then three caress my ear,
Each fluttering like a candle flame—
And Scotch-and-soda is the name.

In the Morning

My head, which is about to split,
Says Scotch-and-soda wasn't *it*.
So many lesser things are prized
Before a man is civilized,
That only bee and Hottentot
May understand the apricot.

The camel looks a bit distorted;
The fecund rabbit rather thwarted—
For Nature's laws are sometimes brittle,
Too much bedevils like too little—
The monstrous elephant moronic;
The quilly porcupine platonic;
The exemplary ant, alas,
Seems just a microscopic ass,
Considering how he must pant
And sweat and strive to be an ant;
The eagle has a savage beak
Which none (I hope) presumes to tweak,
Whereas the sparrow, small and shoddy,
Is hissed and boo'd by everybody;
Slick moons on humid summer nights
Promote the primitive delights,
When desperate rich and hopeful poor
Serve that Paris wench *l'amour*;
The river runs into the sea;
The dog into the bustling flea;
The man, tormented and forgot
From birth to earth and who knows what,
Runs into debt, despair and hives,
Needy friends and former wives,
Erosions of the brain and liver
And thence into the Jordan River,

Precisely as he used to do
When Science thought the sky was blue,
And bossy Jahveh thundered through,
And Christ was nothing but a Jew.

The Notebook of a Schnook

schnook = schlemiel

I

I'm sitting home, I feel lonesome,
I feel saber-toothed and ownsome;
If I had a friend of the female gender
I feel I could make the girl surrender.
So I call this one, I call that one,
A bright one, a dim one, a slim one, a fat one,
Till I find a girl who says she's willing
To do the cooing if I do the billing.
So I bill in one place, I bill in another,
And she coos a little, like Whistler's mother;
Then I take her home to my mortgaged chalet,
A cute little place, if not a *palais*,
In a very respectable part of town,
With some rooms upstairs and some down;
I play a record by Tchaikovsky,
A very high-toned approach to lovsky;
   I play waltzes by all the Strausses
And name big names in adjoining houses;
I try etchings, book-ends, brandy,
Rare editions and nougat candy,
Broadloom carpet and rose-leaf ceiling,
On which she can look, I hope, with feeling—

And what happens? You won't believe it;
As usual, nothing—take it or leave it!

II

I write a scenario for moving pictures;
I let myself go without any strictures;
My mind works in bright ascensions;
The characters swell and get dimensions;
The heroine rises from Gimbel's basement
To what could be called a magic casement,
By sheer virtue and, call it pluck,
With maybe a reel and a half of luck;
She doesn't use posterior palsy
Or displace so much as a single falsie;
She scorns the usual oo-la-la
And never ruffles a modest bra,
(The censor's dream of the cinema);
She doesn't find pearls in common oysters;
She sips a little but never roisters.
The hero's gonads are under wraps,
He never clutches or cuffs or slaps
In heat Vesuvian, or even Stygian—
He acts Oxonian or Cantabrigian
With maybe a soupçon of the South—
Cotton wouldn't melt in his mouth;
The plot could harmlessly beguile
A William Wordsworth honey chile;
The Big Shot's hot and the little shotlets
Wake their wives with contagious hotlets.
So what happens? The usual factors—
The studio simply can't get actors,

Directors, cutters, stagehands, stages,
Or girls to type the extra pages:
The way it ends, to put it briefly,
Is what happens is nothing, chiefly.

III

I work hard, I earn little,
A roof, a beer, a vittle, a skittle;
I keep—well what, if you haven't got money
Do you *think* you can keep—a high-class honey,
Maybe a nobleman's youngest daughter
With a yacht to protect her from salt and water?—
I keep a budget, a can of herring,
A box of matzos and maybe swearing.
Well, the worm turns 'round like a fresh-made cruller,
He's now a horse of another color—
I begin to make money, fast and plenty;
Life looks like rainbows and spumenti;
I begin to regard Jehovah highly,
And think of the life of the younger Riley;
I begin to dream of Lucullan doin's:
I'll travel a lot and see the ruins;
I'll hire a butler who doesn't hurry,
Who doesn't work, but who's pure Surrey,
A chauffeur who looks like the late Lord Essex,
A maid with wattles firm and Wessex;
I'll pay, spot cash, three years' advance
And import a cook from Paris, France;
O Paris, France! O Town de luxe!
I see you as you were in books—
O Paris, France, where gay *les femmes*
Cavort and do not give a *demmes*;

312

Where waxed and debonair *les hommes*
Disport and do not give a *dommes;*
Where even merry *les enfants*
Know all and do not give a *dants!*—
I'm running wild, I must subdue
What you could call my parvenu—
Well anyhow, I'm thinking of
La belle amour and even love;
Of serving dinners in ten courses,
And meeting gents who own horses
And powerful, natural female forces
Who own the gents who own the horses—
So what happens? I pay taxes;
The earth wobbles on half an axis;
I'm happy if the butler's cousin
Drops in sometimes for a daily dozen,
If I meet people who fix plumbing,
Or own a goldfish that's up and coming—
Things could happen to guys like Nero,
But to me, excuse the expression, zero.

IV

I paid my taxes. I got sick;
The doctor said I was going quick
Of double multiple complications,
Confirmed by seven consultations.
Well, if this is it, I said, resigned,
I'll do some thinking in my mind,
I'll do some planning in my head
On the way I'll live when they say I'm dead.
Well, first I'll go and get my blessing,
Then take my time about convalescing,

313

Because the sickness that I got
Weakens a fellow quite a lot.
I'll lie around a couple of eons
And listen to them pealing pæans
And drumming on what they call there, tabors,
And get acquainted with the neighbors,
And flop and sprawl on golden grass
And watch the little cherubs pass,
The way, up there, they call their cuties—
And from the pictures are they beauties!—
Sift pearls and rubies through my fingers,
Sing tenor with the carol singers,
And while I'm loafing, maybe lay
Some onyx up for a rainy day.
Then when I'm feeling good and strong
And think that I can live that long—
Because up there you feel immortal
Or else they show you the so-called portal—
I'll move into my permanent mansion,
With grounds enough for later expansion,
Take a look-see 'round the place,
Pick up a little special grace,
Meet the Biggies, make my mark,
Get promoted from angel to arch-,
Or maybe, even this could be,
To seraph, thirty-third degree,
With extra wings. Well, that's about
As far as I got when I passed out.
So what happened? To put it clearly,
Not only nothing, but nothing merely
And absolutely. You won't believe it:
I'm not even an angel—take it or leave it.

Mild Observation

When Genghis Khan, for bloody robe,
Wore one-half the flowing globe,
Nations trembled at his tread
And envied their completed dead.

Now Genghis is a misty name
But mentioned when the young declaim,
And even later horrors seem
Dissolving vapors of a dream.

A little horror now and then
Seems relished by the world of men,
Else, how could it so soon prepare
For newer horrors in the air.

To Joyce Kilmer, Respectfully

'Poems are made by fools like me,
But only God can make a tree"—
So what can fools like me essay
Who cannot make a night or day,
A star, a herring, or a worm,
A mountain or a modest germ,
A lily, lamb, or even fleece,
Or, like the Lord Himself, a peace,
A zephyr or a hurricane,
A zebra, antelope, or rain;
Who cannot even fashion pain?

While God was busy with His tree,
Who made the fools like you and me?
Did He assign some lesser god
To shape us of inferior sod?
Did we slip through some secret door
While branches strewed His workroom floor?

To many, who but dimly see,
Your poem made a flowering tree,
And did not Jesus by Siloam
Make of gentle words a poem
Whereof a tree was born in light
Upon a man's astonished sight?

To a Certain Person

~~~~~~

Within this room we have identity—
God's mark and manumission. Here, no bleak
Fusion of each with all, that none is free.
Here we have self—raped word by which the weak
Exorcise life. Assurance, young and strong,
Walks tall and tender, arm in arm with fate.
Figures emerge from the sweet womb of song.
Here I behold and blithely re-create
Hellenic evenings in your garnet hair.
Here nights, rich-tasting, every hunger slake.
Songs gush from rock. And in this room we dare,
In spite of totems and taboos, to make
The livid world and its factitious doom
A bright extension of this little room.

I. *Boy*

The boy is told to be a man. But why?
For strength, why not the elephant or ox?
The eagle for assurance in the sky?
For grace, the tiger, speed, the hound or fox?

For courage not compact of serried mass
Why not the lion, and the hare for love?
For fortitude the philosophic ass?
For innocence why not the deer or dove?

For patience and humility, the horse?
For publicized distinctiveness, the gnu?
For faith, and will to make of faith a force,
Why not a woman, and for wisdom too?

For peace, why not an oyster or a clam?
For pleasure in his trade, why not a bee?
For some sweet Mary's sake, why not a lamb?
And almost anything for honesty?

The boy is malleable; he may weave
These elements into a noble span—
Is it not said we are what we believe?
Then why this vile and venal thing called man?

Or, if the task be easier, for joy,
Why not adjure him to remain a boy?

II. *Air for the G-String*

The bawdy and busy-ast
Buxom ecdysiast
Grinds and bumps
Her hinter-humps.

The equally asinine
Quasi-masculine
Is delighted
And excited.

And why not?
Sterile motion, sterile deed
And fruitless seed.
Here is his story better told
Than by harsh days of heat and cold.

III. *Wanted*

Wanted—by Dayrise and rosiferous Earth,
By Noon and Afternoon and Evening,
By Trees, Hedges, Bushes, Birds, Grass,
By Justice, and What-Good-May-Come-to-Pass,
By the Solar System, Stellar Universe,
A Person missing in Recorded Time,
Sole Heir of the Sublime,
For the return of these, his Properties,
Now in their keeping—

His Rights, his Mind, Identity and Soul,
Also, his Obligations.

Occupation:
For Battle—
Cattle;
For Peace—
Fleece;
For Life—
Servant of Mass and Myth, Hewer of Hollow Stones;
For Death—
Bones.

Name: Individual Man.

IV. *Metamorphosis*

I used to breathe unexcised air,
Ensorcelled by Circean care,
As bilious, choleric and glum
As folk possessed by Kingdom Come.
Suburbia on a Sunday night
Was not a more forbidding sight—
My brow was creased, my pants were not;
I horrified the cradled tot;
I let my whiskers grow in reams
To thwart the barber in his themes,
And gloated when my stubborn fleece
Annulled his conversation piece;
I glowered at the passerby,
Pooh-pooh'd the sea, the stars, the sky,
Was wont in malice to reflect

With *double entendre, mot* direct,
On roses, robins, hip or breast,
Or anything these might suggest,
And once, with sour and cynic quips,
Refused to look at an eclipse.

And then one night, when I was filled
With thaumaturgic grain, distilled,
Bottled, uncorked, and poured in glass,
A transformation came to pass,
A metamorphosis was wrought
By this horrendous dread and thought:
When my stenotic days were over
My bones would turn to poisoned clover,
Arsenic grass, unfit to chew,
A noxious nut, or maybe two,
Which trusting sparrow, squirrel and cow
Would eat, and say farewell to Now,
Would shuffle off their mortal slips
Because I snubbed a fine eclipse,
Because I was a grouse, a grump,
A churl, a heel, a cad, a chump.
How should I face my honest friends
When Gabriel called to dividends
And all of us together rose
And entered heaven, nose by nose?
My pores ran wild, my hair stood up—
I felt a dirty buttercup.

Now, when my fellow men dismay
Themselves, the earth, and night and day,
And I could look with merry quips

Upon their permanent eclipse,
Or when Jehovah, Jove, or Zeus
Decides I am a cornered moose,
I think of cows upon the munch
Or happy sparrows having lunch
Or furry squirrels at their brunch,
And radiate, effuse, exude,
And even sweat the cheerful mood,
And loose my dentures in a smile,
And walk a lissome quarter-mile,
And say hello to tots and nurses,
And mull some amiable verses,
And do not think of folk I pass
As noxious nuts or poisoned grass.

I wish there were a conscious movement
Among the beasts for our improvement.

V. *Derivative Quatrain. Discovered on a Wall of the Author's Attic*

Tax me not in mournful numbers,
Come and make a total haul,
For the residue that slumbers
Is no good to me at all.

VI. *Fragment—on the Thought That an Infant Might One Day Seek Public Office: A Lullaby*

Potential Menace, cooing in your Crib,
For all I know, the Embryonic Fib,

The Nascent Whopper or Rococo Word
By which to hypnotize the Ovine Herd,
Now in liquescent Diaper strait confined,
But possibly for Leadership designed,
For Head or Tail or Maw or Claw of State,
Rehearsing now to lie or liquidate,
Harass, confuse, betray, appeal or beg—
My Minatory Twig, my Serpent Egg,
Rockabye. . . .

VII. *Balmy Ooze with Bryophytes*

The hippopotamus delights
In balmy ooze with bryophytes,
Whereon he lolls and sprawls and snoozes
And, being one with Nature, oozes,
Snorting a lush and mighty breath
And seeming unprepared for death,
While Man, serenity eschewing,
Is always up and down and doing,
For aqueous days a painful sieve,
Equipped to die but not to live.
Sadly I weigh the hippo's gains
Against my few and scattered brains,
His hide against my shirt and pants,
His fleas against my massive ants,
And choose the ooze and water-plants.

VIII. *Song for the Flute*

O, dear familiar of my heart,
So gracious, fair and kind,

Would you could lose your other part
Of stranger to my mind.

O, would that Reason were as blind
As Love, or had the art
Of seeming pleasantly resigned,
Or feigning the fierce dart.

From deserts of the wise I start
Toward You, my love, and find
The dearest substance of my heart,
A shadow of my mind.

IX. *Thorn Song*

Talent in evil
Ends on the gallows,
But genius in evil
Avoids the shallows,
Rides currents high and free
And fashions heroes for humanity.

X. *Wilderness*

The wilderness which only storms caress,
Seas from the living world a void apart,
May drain a deeper, icier loneliness
Out of the human heart.

XI. *Question and Answer*

What is so rare as a day in June?
Decent behavior
From a popular savior.

"It Is Finished"

~~~~~~

He said, It is finished: and He bowed
His Head and gave up the ghost. John 19:30

No, Lord, it is not finished. You are still
Transfixed upon the wood, the world your hill;
The spear has lengthened to the branching spire;
The crown become humanity on fire,
Burning Your brow with fiercer pain than thorn,
With hate more piercing than the Roman scorn.
The mourners at Your feet are very few.
It is not finished, till a sunrise new
Strike from the minds of men the wounds that bleed,
And leave them gasping at the Word, the Deed.

For a Zither

~~~~~~~~~~~~~~~~~~~~~~~~~~~~~~~~~~~~~~~

These things are eternally true
To the memory of you:
An empty vase that held your rose,
Books that only you may close,
Doors that let you go, whose wood
Is wistful with my solitude,
A lonely lamp with shade awry,
As if it struggled not to cry,
As if some shade-born hope said "wait,"
And you would come to set it straight.
The very silence 'round these things
Of a remembered motion sings,
Motion you gave to them and grace
And in our heaven their starry place:
These things kept the vows we made,
These things were true, and we betrayed.

Churchbells

When I was a little lad
Sunday churchbells made me sad,
Made me wish I hadn't been
Born a Jew and deep in sin,
For as many a Christian boy
Told me with unChristly joy
I had personally done
A thing to blacken sky and sun,
In hate and malice sacrificed
His Lord and Saviour, Jesus Christ,
And though, since I was barely ten,
I couldn't quite remember when
I had done the hellish thing,
I used to hear the churchbells ring,
And dogs of terror scampered blind
Through Ghetto alleys of my mind,
And barked in bells from Christian spires,
And ran in rings 'round Christian fires,
And crucifixes, wild of eye,
On their single legs strode by.

I watched the people, still and strange,
Passing in their Sunday change,
Knife-lipped women, rock-faced men,
Seemingly the same as when
I saw them every other day,

Yet skies and seas and lands away,
And felt forlorn and child-alone,
And felt that way among my own—
No Gentile dark with love of Christ
Whom I and mine had sacrificed,
No Jew with skullcap on his head
Mumbling something Moses said—
A leaf that fluttered from no tree,
Nor came to rest, nor yet was free,
A tree that walked, but never grew,
A living semblance, but a Jew,
Lost in the United States,
Lost behind the Ghetto gates,
No bird, yet wingless, lost in air,
Alone and alien everywhere.

Now I am a large and mellow,
Mild and philosophic fellow
Of amiable thought and speech,
Sweetly disposed toward all and each,
A stanch disciple of Saint Paul,
A friend of sparrows as they fall,
Contained, reflective and resigned,
Of equable Franciscan mind,
Content with almost anything,
I hear the Sunday churchbells ring
Upon a morning broad and bright,
And think the little lad was right
And *will* be till the gods unite
And One God says, "Let there be light!"

Stanzas

The hoptoad hops from here to there
And then from there to here,
If he has business anywhere
He does not make it clear,
And yet, I notice, when he stops
He seems intent on further hops.

A purpose surely lies in these
Concatenated jumpings,
Divine, as in the buzzing bee's
Persistent flower-thumpings;
Or up, of course, a few gradations,
The hoppy history of nations.

Weather Report

I. *Freudian Footnote*

I love my love because she's fair
And has a cold-wave in her hair;
Because her lips and handbags match
And she's considered quite a catch;
Because she has the winsome ways
Of waiters in the best cafés;
Dependable as Holland gin,
I always know whose bed she's in,
So purely flustered when she lies,
Three times I've doubted my own eyes;
Because she listens with a look
Of violets by a babbling brook,
As bright and beautiful as they,
As sensitive to what I say—
But most, this shiny suit I press
Because for *me* I care much less.

II. *Emendation*

When lovely woman stoops to rise
In furs and jewels to the eyes,
Call it any kind of folly,
You cannot make her melancholy!

III. *Thought While Serving on a Jury*

When I was young in that green time
Between B.C. and now,
And rhymed to live and lived to rhyme
And loved the girls like chow,
And thoughts of what I *couldn't* get
Disturbed not what I got,
And life was like the alphabet,
Why, I was young—so what?

IV. *Parlor Game*

Who pays and pays and pays? The woman
Humanly frail, divinely human!
Who pays the woman? The paying teller!
Who pays the teller? Oh, just some feller!

V. *The Forest of Arden*

An epoch writhes and dies,
But in the nightclubs and shops
The glamor-girls glitter and twitter
And peck at slops.

VI. *For the Harmonica*

When in course of time you see,
In place of an illusion, me,
Please remember that you cozen'd
Me into the man I wasn't.

332

He, by that time, being dead,
Give your heart to me, instead;
You may find, to your surprise,
A faint resemblance in the eyes!

VII. *Soliloquy While Waiting*

Never let your passion rise
To your head or to the skies;
Confine it to protective pants
Along with sundry other ants;
A cheerier world, a greener earth
Is bought with, say, three buttons' worth.

VIII. *Composed on the Beach at Santa Monica*

Constant as the climate,
Fickle as the weather,
We shall be eternally,
Capriciously together.

IX. *Song for Election Day*

Winter, or spidery Spring,
Summer, or cidery Fall,
Whatever my fortune may bring,
Je suis un derrière du cheval.

Do not too hastily spring
Therefore, poor *me* to condemn;
Whatever *your* fortune may bring—
Tu, mon ami, es le même.

Drums

Lying in the dark I hear,
Shaken with wonder, cold with fear,
The tiny drumbeats of my heart
Play their incessant, fatal part.

Two billion hearts, by day and night,
Drum down the shade, drum up the light,
Drum seasons up to tend the tree,
Drum strength and sound into the sea,
Drum Death out of Eternity.

The Forest

You cast the deed so lightly on the stream
Of Time, and think it lightly flows away;
You cast the word so lightly to the day,
These pledges that you never can redeem
If at some fatal moment in the scheme
Of life you may have need of them again—
The deed that might have sheltered you from pain,
The word that might have saved another's dream.
You are no solitary tree that stands
And drops its leaves upon a barren place,
But one whose leaves and branches interlace
A multitude with living hearts and hands:
The same life sings in you that sings in these,
And babbles of immense antiquities.

Mid-May Song

~~~~~~

Now mid-May's here and I contrive
To add two twos and make them five.
Meanwhile, the loud, mammalian earth
Imbues with her priapic mirth
The hippopotamus and flea,
The queer baboon, the cruising bee,
The caterpillar on the tree,
The proud giraffe (who knows that he
Is modern architecturally)—
Imbues, in short, with springtime all
The Kingdom of the Animal,
Save one, whose maladjusted span
Constitutes the Life of Man.

While birds toot sweet on every bough,
And grass-grown yearnings fill the cow
With milk (grade A), and even cream,
And things are maybe what they seem,
And chickens, tipsy with the May,
Lay and lay and lay and lay
And lay (lay off; go on from here!)
And jolly mid-May flies appear,
In perfect harmony with all
On which they chance to light or fall,
And more successful upside down
Than any leading man in town—

While this occurs, and even more,
From shore to (naturally) shore,
And tick and tiger, bee and bear
Make vernal whoopee everywhere,
The lord of Science and the Arts,
Self-sung for various noble parts—
No less than Man himself I mean—
Continues to perplex the scene
And make the startled spring go boom
With antic gesta hominum;
With isms, schisms, cults and creeds;
With febrile itches, phantom needs;
With saws and laws and cant and prayer;
With graft and craft and greed and care;
With freakish use and monster skill;
With idiot goal and maniac will;
With spires and swords and leagues and wars
And surfs of talk on sandy shores;
With in hoc signo on a Sunday
And caveat emptor, starting Monday;
With sour achieving, harried striving,
Belly pacts and spleen conniving,
With—halt! survey the dimpled sight,
And catalogue your own delight.

Of all who labored from the slime
Under the dogged feet of Time,
While past slipped into crackling past,
Is this, is Man, the first or last?
Has not the ape contrived to reach
Beyond the barren buttes of speech,
Beyond the quicksands of the mind

(His serio-comic world behind),
A pride, a place, a peace more stanch
In his plain Heaven of a branch?
Has not the tree itself attained
Its topmost powers, and stands ordained
In priesthood of harmonious place?
Before it found an equal grace,
What conquered worlds behind the bird
Of cactus Deed and tidal Word?
Is not, most ancient of the stock,
The rock melodious to the rock
Of human woes and human pains
Remembered in its empty veins?
Is there no wisdom wiser than
The fret, the fear, the whine of Man?

Well, mid-May's here and I contrive
To add two twos and keep alive,
And ponder Plato, now a fly,
Upon his ceiling of a sky.

Song, on Reading that the Cyclotron Has Produced Cosmic Rays, Blasted the Atom into Twenty-two Particles, Solved the Mystery of the Transmutation of Elements and Devil Knows What

Be gay, be merry, and don't be wary of milking the
    modest minute;
Rollick and frolic and carpe diem for all the fun
    that's in it;
Gather roses, or rose-red noses, and samba the night
    away:
There's nothing to fear but life and death—as far
    as we know today.

The lads in the lab are in high confab and the gods
    are huddled in holes;
There's a murmuration of trepidation among estab-
    lished souls;
The atom's groggy, the future foggy, so join your
    doggie at play:
There's nothing to fear but life and death—as far
    as we know today.

There's rootin' and tootin' in stellar spaces and secret
    places therein;
The mild professors are now possessors of something
    stronger than gin;

Before the payoff let's take a layoff and all be queens
    of the May:
There's nothing to fear but life and death—*as far
    as we know today!*

The rights of each are the only rights of all.

Eve grinned before the fall.

The malevolent tyrant destroys; the benevolent tyrant humiliates.

Man proposes; woman affiliates.

Wherever the worm turns, he is still a worm.

Power never serves too brief a term.

Where there are willing masters there are willing slaves.

Where there are mass men there are mass graves.

Only the obligations of the strong assure the rights of the weak.

Envy is the mistress of the meek.

Marriages made in Heaven are not exported.

A fool and his money are soon courted.

When the ox has wings, the eagle will draw the cart.

The taste of another's luck is always tart.

Who shouts of his labor covets another's yield.

What God confided to the clergy has never been revealed.

A wrong to one outlaws the State.

Free to worship still means free to hate.

Where the mighty swarm, God is hidden.

Joy is the most forbidden.

Real wealth is the soul in repose.

Thorns do not impede the rose.

Where one is nothing, all are nothing.

Beware of a dog and a saviour frothing.

"No" is a giant's word.

Parents should be seen, but children heard.

The body cannot give itself pleasure.

Work is the fig-leaf of leisure.

Who governs himself cheats the State.

Faith condones, Courage despises, Fate.

The wages of sin are high.

The half-truth is the cancer of the lie.

Every man's poverty adds to the demagogue's wealth.

Few reach high office save by stealth.

The lying servant becomes the brutal master.

Only One God is not made of plaster.

No taxation without misrepresentation.

Geography never made a nation.

Who robs Peter will never pay Paul.

The thirst of the great is the drink of the small.

The wealth of the world will be redistributed with its brains.

To starve more slowly, starve on another's gains.

No man should be called common except by his cook.

We need more cooks.

No man is fit, by law or wit, or custom, suffrage or intent, or hazard, need or accident, to rule another than himself, save from the gallows or the shelf.

Wisdom bears buds, Virtue, blossoms, Force, fruit.

On the hog mind, assurance is the snoot.

To a woman, experience means love; to a man, traffic tickets.

Simple Saint Peter stays outside the wickets, knowing, as *he* does, by his own belief, the stinkweed has become immortal leaf, and the starved mind and heart eternal rickets.

So long—and yet, so short, for this life's grievance and the snort.

~~~~~~

I. *Moses*

Below him Canaan glittered like a shield;
He saw the land beneath the burning sun
And dreamed its milk and honey field by field:—
Not bitterly he knew his work was done
And laid in misty Death's that mighty hand.
He sat upon a rock and gazed; the Lord,
Standing beside him, spake: "Behold, the land
That I have promised unto Joshua's sword,
Unto my children, Israel, for a crown!"
He gazed on Canaan and he shed no tears—
The burden of his people weighed him down;
The weariness of all those desert years.
He smiled a little before he fell asleep
Thinking how he had sowed and who shall reap.

II. *Joshua*

"Moses, my servant, is dead." So spake the Lord,
Laying a hand all warm with love and sun
Upon the shoulders of the son of Nun,
"And I shall keep with thee my promised Word!"
And Joshua fumbled at his girded sword,
For on his arm the hand of Israel's God
Was trembling like a grass-blade in the sod.

The mighty Captain plucked his garment's cord,
And dared not look upon the Face that spake,
Hearing a Voice that wavered like a flame
Before the mention of His servant's name.
He thought the Heart of God would surely break,
And looked out tearfully upon his clan;
The Lord of Wrath was weeping like a man.

To a Friend, B.J., Age, Six Months

Hello, Fats!
Hello, Smiler!
Four-bottle Man and Unaware Beguiler!
Philosopher without philosophy;
No prophet, but Incarnate Prophecy
Of something hunky-dory and okay
That's on the way
And will arrive one day, or any day!
I seem to see you wink an eye,
Bump a shoulder against the sky
Confidentially,
As if to say, *"They'll* see."
Hello, you Dimpled Future, Shriver of the Past,
Recaster of all things miscast,
Sayer—I hear you, though no word is said,
No sign, save a small rumple on the bed
And sundry hollows—
Of this, as follows:
"We are not shaped for grief or hate or wrong,
But fruitful labor, happy love and song
And innocence and fellowship and joy."
Hello, Boy!
You, who are still with sunrise, answer this:
What's gone amiss?
Aha—I see; I'm sure I saw you nod
Again, as follows: "We ourselves, not God—

347

And God another name for what we are,
Not something far beyond the farthest star."
Well, thanks, Fats!
Thanks, Smiler!
Real Wise Guy!
Small Beguiler!

Personal Notation

~~~~~~

At night, when you *should* sleep, you can't sleep yet;
By day, when you shouldn't, you laugh at sheep yet;
Things you're expecting, they get aphasia;
Things you're avoiding fly over from Asia;
If you want to go out, you could tear your hair yet,
You could even break dishes, and not think where yet;
If you want to stay in, a dozen people
Bang at the phone like bats in a steeple;
If you feel fine, from toe to cranium
You look like a relic of Herculaneum;
If you feel sick, you look sturdy—
So what will the end be? Well, where is Verdi?

If you like a girl, she likes biceps,
Regular he-men and even triceps,
Which you don't get from wrestling verses
Or playing checkers with night nurses;
If you meet a girl whom God forgot yet,
She wants to protect you from Heaven knows what
     yet;
If you want to cavort and sing and laugh yet,
The party's a meeting of Chiefs of Staff yet;
If you feel the way a mortician looks yet,
They get so gay they drag in the cooks yet;
Loafers eat while you stay broke yet—
So what will the end be? Ask James K. Polk yet!

349

If you like birds, you'll live in New York yet,
Where children arrive without even a stork yet;
If you think a lark is a loud-mouthed weevil,
You're sure to commute to a forest primeval;
If you want a world at least as bearable
As it was in the time of Ivan the Terrible,
They begin to prepare for a deadlier war yet
To exterminate all, and even more yet;
If you feel relaxed at such release yet,
They turn around and threaten peace yet—
So what will the end be? Well, read the papers
In a million years, and compare the capers.

A *Simple Tale*

I had a girl and *you* had a girl
And she was a pretty dame,
And mine was mine and yours was yours
And she was one and the same.

Yes, *I* had a girl and *you* had a girl
And she had a lovely laugh,
And whenever *I* saw her, whenever *you* saw her,
We always sawed her in half.

Now *she* has a fellow, a loving fellow,
But a careworn fellow and pale,
Who wonders which of us got the head
And which of us got (a simple tale),
And which of us got the other part,
And which of us got, in short, her heart.

Practical Conclusion

~~~~~~

This is the better way for us, my dear,
This pleasant and convenient compromise;
I should have lost you had you seen me clear
With innocent or unremembering eyes.

But, as it is, substantially I please,
Observed, while some subconscious dream abets,
Through stained-glass windows of your memories,
Or camellia-mists of your subdued regrets.

Obituary

When a body is broken
Something is shaken
From all things that are—
A face, a garden, a God, a star.

The sun will not be less
In strength, or night in tenderness;
They will be just as flawless, just as fair,
But something that was there will not be there.

The moon will be as shimmering and as bright
As when, on one vast, sea-receding night,
She taught the nascent eye to utter light.

But she will know in her mercurial soul
That she is not as whole.

For I was one string on a dulcimer
That sang her radiant beauty back to her.
My eye that held her majesty was seen
In dark she could not enter, being queen.

For each holds the stars in their courses
And each holds a God on His throne,
And the life that goes into darkness
Always takes back its own.

Fantasy on a Familiar Theme

I shot an arrow into the air,
It fell to earth and I knew where;
It fell like a plummet, swift and free,
Into the U.S. Treasury.

I breathed a song into the air
And thought it would find a landing there;
But down it went, like a skiff at sea,
Into the U.S. Treasury.

I tossed my labor into the air
To scatter the crows of fear and care;
Down it came, but not to me—
Into the U.S. Treasury.

I threw a statesman into the air;
The world and weather changed to fair;
But down he dropped, like a drunken bee,
Into the U.S. Treasury.

I hurled the Treasury into the air;
I blasted it while it hovered there;
I muttered a prayer, I said a grace—
And there it stood in the same old place.

Advice to the Lovelorn
(Women Only)

~~~~~~

Great oaks from little acorns grow;
Ah, would in life the rule were so!
What has the little acorn got
That papa's eager seed has not?

Before the cracking nations fail,
The acorn must supplant the male;
Before the world goes up in smoke,
Ladies, get yourselves with oak!

Quatrain

The night climbs upward toward the eternal past;
The silence gnaws at the silent heart like a mouse;
Patience! After so many deaths the last
Is only the locking of an empty house.

Quiz

Do you now refer to fun as folly,
Enjoy night-rising and melancholy?
Is your mind vague and uninspired?
Is your sense of integer vitae tired?
Do your legs ache, does your memory creak?
Do you work an hour and rest a week?
Do you sit in the sun when you should be swimmin'?
Does your middle suggest a ripe persimmon?
(Are you glad I didn't rhyme swimmin' with women?)
Do you snort, eruct and sound alarming
When you want to be urbane and charming?
Do you read tales of wild adventure
While you try to dock a floating denture?
Do you absently reach for your noble dome
And find you're holding a useless comb?
Do you have symptoms—spots, itches,
No sense of shame without your britches?
Do you store milk, bicarb of soda
Instead of Scotch in your front pagoda?
Do you look at your wife and remember clearly
That for thirty years you've loved her dearly
With never a twitch for any other,
Pat her shoulder and call her mother?
Well, think of all that was before,
The call to arms in peace or war,
The dates, the parties, jobs and worry,

The itch for sports and scampering hurry,
The haircuts, shaves, shampoos and shines,
The pressings, postures, smirks and lines,
The being alert and still on guard
To win a word or brief regard,
The smoking torches that you carried
Before and after you were married,
The envy, jealousy, fear and spite,
The morning after the maudlin night,
The urgings, purgings, scourgings of
The tender mind in life and love,
And if you're not content with what
You've got, you may think you're old—you're not;
You're full of cold and half-baked beans;
You're in your demi- and semi-teens;
You're quasi-nubile and baby-fat—
And you've got something there, at that.

To a Cat

If Peace and Silence could arise
And walk, and look with living eyes,
And Night her starry cross descend
And stretch herself and be my friend
For shrimps and beef—I'm certain that
They'd be yourself, imperial cat!

You shame of all your jungle sires,
Of tiger-lords and panther-squires,
Well may these mighty warriors spare
To my distress your royal air—
I to my species, you to theirs
Apostate in adjoining chairs.

Here in this quiet room we dream
Amendments to the primal scheme:
You in your feline terms, of ease,
Catnip, and such urbanities;
I, of a jungle strength to dare to
Smite the three-score ills I'm heir to!

Who Grope, With Love for Hands

Who grope, with love for hands, outstretched to light,
Will break their fumbling fingers on a wall.
In that fierce flash of pain the wise see all—
The nested robin and the nested sea,
The silent brood-hen of Eternity,
Marbled in azure that nor speaks nor sings—
And nest their souls beneath those flightless wings.

Portrait

~~~~~~

Nothing is quite so much in clover
As ancient dames, who grandly sit,
Broad in the beam and beam all over,
At one with every bit of it.

They love assorted nephews, nieces,
Cousins of immemorial date;
The world around them goes to pieces—
But hour by hour they integrate.

And one day they will see Death hover
About the door respectfully,
And, as they would a timid lover,
Wave him in for cakes and tea.

Description

You are no compromise with any dream;
You and the violent world, the actual sun,
The vivid sea, the racing quinquereme,
Struggle, defeat and victory are one.

You are no unguent for diseased regrets,
Those stricken sparrows with the broken wings;
Hermaphrodite of shabby violets
Hid in the attics of forgotten springs.

You are no pale, compensatory shape
That haunts the porch of the surrendered soul;
No dim, nocturnal alley of escape;
No far mirage the wretched call a goal.

No dream that was, no vision that might be
Can decimate your strong reality.

Postlude

~~~~~~

The next world war was over and done and so was
    the human race;
The stag at bay was at bay no more as he lolled in his
    rilly place;
The pigeon strolled in the rubble heaps with assured
    and easy air,
Or stopped for a chat with a jungle cat or a word with
    a loafing bear.

There was peace at last in the animal world, there was
    peace in the fishful sea;
There was peace on earth, there was peace in time,
    there was peace in Eternity;
The tree was free of the pain of the axe, the earth of
    the pain of the plough,
And she smiled as she suckled the stalwart steer, the
    deer, the sheep and the cow.

It was pleasant indeed when the sun went down and
    the animals walked the sod,
And the birds flew forth and the fish leaped up for
    an evening chat with God,
And the young moon twinkled merrily and glimmered
    a silver glee:
"How nice it is to shine upon such elegant company!"

It was pleasant indeed when the sun came up and the
     animals stirred the sod,
And the parrot rode on the camel's back for a morn-
     ing word with God,
And the young sun twinkled merrily and glimmered a
     golden glee:
"How nice it is to shine upon such charming com-
     pany!"

For the Lord Himself came down for a walk, smoking
     a blue cigar,
And the end of it twinkled contentedly, like the morn-
     ing and evening star;
He said "hello" to the eagle and mole and the animals
     far and near,
And the whale and the bass swam close to shore and
     stood on their tails to hear.

He leaned against the firmament and He didn't look
     Big at all;
He looked like all that there was to see, and that can
     be very small;
He leaned against the firmament and threw His cigar
     away,
And the hawk swooped down and the sparrow up, to
     hear what He had to say.

"Well, folks," He said, as He shook His head and
     paused for a zephyr breath,
"The Pest that pestered us One and all has pestered
     himself to death;

364

It wasn't *My* Will that did him in, it wasn't *My* High
    Command,
For, whatever it was, the Thing I made has long been
    out of Hand.

"You lived in beautiful amity with Me, and each with
    each,
Until I set the Creature down upon the primal beach;
I wasn't quite sure what the Thing might be, when
    first I set him free,
For this was a new experiment in Heavenly Chemistry.

"There was one part I and one part you and a part
    that came to Me,
In a dream that lasted a million years, of a new
    Eternity,
And I wondered whether I could or couldn't, and
    then I resolved I could—
But I didn't know My Chemistry as well as the Good
    Lord should.

"Now you are folks I am glad I made, for all of you
    came out clean:
I never mistook a moose for a mouse or a hornèd toad
    for a deer;
I knew you all by sight and smell and stripe and beak
    and fur,
And I knew how to rule and regulate, for I knew what
    your natures were.

"But This was Something that wasn't you and I'm
    sure that he wasn't I;

He didn't seem to belong on land, in water or air or
    sky;
He fought, bewildered, confused, corrupted My crea-
    tures of soil and sea;
He blocked and battled, dismayed, confused, and cer-
    tainly baffled Me.

"I tried to contain him with threats and gifts, to con-
    trol and appease and abate;
He left Me no time to evolute *you* to a more en-
    lightened state;
He taught you to trample by his example the laws of
    the Ought and Must—
Well, I've chalked him down in devil red in column
    B for Bust.

"But part of his fault was *My* Own Fault, and part of
    his want and woe,
So part of his dust will be quiet dust and part of the
    peace you know;
The young who died with unsweetened mouths I will
    make into honey-bees,
And the fragrant children who never lived shall be
    my lilac trees.

"I will make an acre of earth and time of the simple,
    the humble, the good,
And let them utter their whiteness forth in the white
    of the birchen wood;
And those who wanted only to sing, their death is a
    piercing wrong:

366

I will make of their dust a peachtree switch that they
      find their spring of song.

"I will make of some a rememberance like a voiceless
      voice in the night;
And some I will keep in My eyes forever and make
      them part of My sight;
Of the rest I will make a Never Was and turn them
      out of My Past;
I will turn them into a Dream again—a Bigger Dream
      than the last."

He stopped and stepped with a single stride into the
      massive blue;
The heron stood on a single leg as he does in the eve-
      ning slough;
The whale remained on his mighty tail, where the
      tangled tide was caught;
The tall giraffe leaned on a palm, and thought and
      thought and thought.

There was peace at last in the animal world, there
      was peace in the fishful sea;
There was peace on earth, there was peace in time,
      there was peace in Eternity;
There was peace in the East and peace in the West
      and peace in the cobalt span;
There was peace at last in the fading ruins, and peace
      in the heart of Man.

To My Mother

O Mother, with the beautiful, still eyes
These many years dissolved into the earth,
Who never ceased to give my being birth,
You cannot see now from your crumbled grave
Or through the eyes of the dispassionate stars,
How little even your tenderness could save
My own life from the doom of all men's lives.
Or did you, in the long night silentness
Foresee it all, and weep, that for your love
You took me from the realm of the unborn,
And set me, with a kiss and with a tear,
Upon the road that all men walk with Christ
Unto the thorns, the nails, the rending spear?

To get the smell of bread and roses;
Dingle's boy is going to college—
He always had a thirst for knowledge;
He says he wants to build a bridge
From Laurel Hill to Warrior Ridge;
My missus makes gefüllte fish
So good you want to eat the dish,
And beef with barley on the bone
That when you eat you kind of moan . . ."
He paused, a veil upon his phiz—
"And that's about the way it is."

I brushed the barley from my brain
And thus addressed my friend again—
"My friend," said I, "I see the scene,
I know exactly what you mean.
Your algebra has mastered all:
Into each rain some life must fall,
As into beer some luckless fly;
Tomorrow, friend, it may be I—
But, till I hear my special drum,
I'm taking no viaticum;
I'm tending to my little garden
And asking no man's pence or pardon,
And sharing, as I have to share,
But not a brussels sprout to care.
The world's a weed, as well I know,
And rankles where you let it grow,
And since begat begat begat,
Is always falling on its pratt
And crushing folk beneath the drear
Expanse of its capricious rear

Eclogue

My heart leaped up when I beheld
A friend of mine named Katzenfeld,
A man as simple as a dish
Of ham and eggs or chips and fish,
Or a geranium in a pot,
Or the unbaptized Hottentot,
Or gentle hiccups gently rumpling
The dreams of the ingested dumpling,
Or Brooklyn as it is today,
Or shining farmers making hay,
Or slanting orchards in the rain,
Or slanting wenches in champagne,
Or Russians rumbling *ochi chornya*
By swimming pools in California,
Or cuties gazing on a book
With long, Laodicean look,
Or sparrows nibbling at a lawn,
Or pigeons gargling up the dawn,
Or lovely ladies advertised
As willing and deodorized,
Or aviators flying fast
As rumor through the startled vast,
Arriving, bold and handsome men,
In time to fly right back again,
Or horses eating oats galore,
Or men at peace, or peace at war,

Or puppies yipping just to yip
Because their hearts are young and flip
And sounding quite by accident
Precisely like a Great Event,
Or measles, marigolds, and mumps,
Or sitting on contented rumps.

I sat him down to honest beer
And thought of many a yesteryear,
And watched a thirst, too proud to halt,
Enschnozzle foam and gurgle malt;
"Oh, friend," said I, and "Friend," I said,
"A blessing on your balding head;
Enjoy your lager while you may—
Tomorrow is a tougher day.
The world, while you inhale your hops,
Is wobbling on its malaprops,
Is dimming out and failing fast
And falling on its mizzenmast,
Is full of bombs and soviets,
Diurnal snorts, nocturnal sweats
And frantic people in gazettes,
Of brambles, scrambles and luctations,
Brabbles, scrabbles, creeds and nations,
Babbling, braying, bruiting, chirping,
Rumbling, bumbling, mumbling, burping,
Cramps and spasms in its drain,
Fissions in its cellophane,
Boiling pundits in its fissions—
And may not last three more editions."
I fixed him with a humid eye—
"Give out, my friend, and prophesy."

He pondered ceiling, pondered wall,
And thus addressed us, one and all—
"The river snoozes through the valley;
The well still stands in Rooster's Alley;
The boys play ball in Dugan's Lane
And scatter when they hit a pane;
The way the sparrows peck the ground
You'd think that horses were around;
The kids squeeze mud between their toes
And Jake is going to marry Rose;
The plums are ripe on Chestnut Street;
The cantaloupes are special sweet;
Gelb, the glazier, talks and talks
And eats a herring as he walks;
Lilacs fell on Lizzie's hat
While standing by the fence to chat;
In Golden's garden, apple leaves
And fireflies are thick as thieves;
In spring and summer, after dark,
There's goings-on in Harvey's Park;
Free lunch is back in all the bars;
My nephew knows the names of stars;
Luke the Loafer's mother died
And for once he really cried,
Told Mrs. Pugh and Mrs. Hassel
He felt like a deserted castle;
Bauer's yard is full of pups;
The fields are nuts with buttercups;
At night the culm-banks glow like stoves
And bakers shovel out fresh loaves
And people, swatting flies in droves,
Turn their heads, expand their noses

And getting up and reeling on
And spoiling eve and shaming dawn.
Henceforth, it's falling on its own—
We'll have some beef upon the bone."

My friend he smiled a smile so faint
It seemed to marry is to ain't;
The sun was drowsing on his head
As, "That's the way it is," he said.